To Cress

Keep jamming

In Business For Yourself

Also by Bruce Williams:
   The Bruce Williams Source Book
   America Asks Bruce

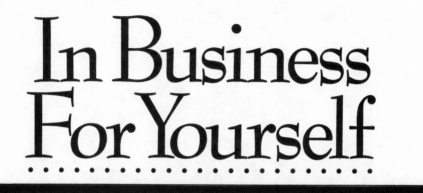

In Business For Yourself

Bruce Williams

WITH WARREN SLOAT

Scarborough House/*Publishers*

Scarborough House/*Publishers*
Lanham, MD 20706

FIRST PUBLISHED IN 1991
Fifth printing 1993

Library of Congress Cataloging-in-Publication Data

Williams, Bruce, 1932-
   In business for yourself / Bruce Williams with
   Warren Sloat.
     p. cm.
   Includes index.
   ISBN 0-8128-4011-9
   1. New business enterprises. 2. Small business.
   I. Sloat, Warren. II. Title.
HD62.5.W493   1991
658' .041—dc20   90-25558
                                CIP

CONTENTS

Introduction 1
1. Rules of Thumb 13
2. Getting Started 29
3. Skills and Trades 51
4. Franchises 69
5. Start-Up Money 81
6. Which Way to Go? 99
7. The Seven Mules: Part I 109
8. The Seven Mules: Part II 127
9. Coping with a Complex Society 149
10. Operating Your Business 167
11. Record-Keeping 181
12. Buying and Pricing 193
13. Marketing 207
14. Shrinkage 221
15. Growth 233
16. The Telephone and Other Tools 243
17. Good Luck 257
Index 263

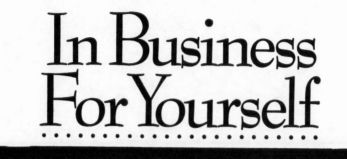

INTRODUCTION

Five nights a week I take off from my New Jersey home and drive into Manhattan. I do a telephone talk show from New York City, the center of the broadcast world, from which we reach the entire Western Hemisphere. Currently the program is heard on about 343 radio stations in the United States, Canada, and the Caribbean area. To make the thing fly, we have set up telephone numbers by means of which callers can reach me toll-free for advice on life.

Happily, my listeners number in the millions. My callers number in the hundreds of thousands. The themes are various, but one emerges as a heavy interest area. It seems universal among people of every age, region, sex, income level, and ethnic group.

One way I've heard it put is negative: "I'm fed up with working for someone else, even though the money is good."

Another way might be: "I want to get into business for myself but I don't know how."

A more positive way of expressing it might be: "I have a great idea that I'd like to develop as an enterprise for myself."

Sometimes the chief motivation is getting rich. Hey, there's nothing wrong with that; I've been preoccupied with getting rich most of my life. Sometimes other factors are involved, such as more satisfaction in work. I don't care if you make a million dollars a year, if going to work is painful, you're underpaid. Sometimes the caller has been in business for himself in the past and wants to get back into it again. Sometimes they're a couple looking for a supplement to an already-existing job—the two-paycheck family is more the style than the exception these days. Some have already plunged into business for themselves and are floundering, because they didn't think it through at the outset.

Some envision a new kind of career that will fulfill them and replace a job that hampers them; while others want to do the same thing they're doing now, but do it for themselves and take the profit themselves. Many are excited about the prospect of setting their own hours, arranging their own agendas, and making their own decisions.

Some see their entrepreneurial venture as a way of "doing my own thing," or as Sinatra puts it, "doing it my way." We're told as children to be independent, to be individuals; yet when you work for someone else, you're not really independent, you're not individual, and frequently it's not to your advantage to act as an individual. When you work for a big organization you are a tiny, albeit integral, part of that organization. Often you feel lost in the shuffle. No wonder so many people want to be the boss and dream of self-employment.

If you want to test this thesis, if you want to see how important a topic it has become, go to a cocktail party, or a pancake breakfast, any social occasion at all, and work it into the conversation. You'll be surprised to find how many people want to get into business for themselves. That's why I decided to write this book—to help you do it if you really want to get beyond just talking about it.

Not Like Big Business

Despite this obvious interest, our newspapers and magazines and academic studies always seem to concentrate on big business. Small business in a number of ways operates on principles completely different from those of big business.

I recently overheard a conversation at a big corporation where a little mistake had been made and the budget had to be increased by another $90,000 because a piece of equipment had been overlooked in budgeting. That would send many a small business right down the toilet. In that same office we discussed another ancillary enterprise, with a profit projection of almost a million dollars, that was going to be scrubbed because sales did not meet expectations. That kind of miscalculation would also destroy the average small enterprise. A small operation cannot tolerate the slippage that is taken for granted in big companies.

I also sat in on a meeting in a large enterprise during which the president was meeting with top executives. One of the executives said, "We've got a serious problem. It takes us six weeks to order a box of paper clips through our procurement system. How do we overcome that?" And the president, a million-dollar-a-year executive, said, "I wish I had an answer. I don't know how to get through that bureaucracy either." Can you imagine a small business that could wait six weeks for anything?

My Experience

Anyway, to get back to the subject, there's a lack of solid information about small business. I have something to offer in this respect, because I've spent most of my life as an entrepreneur. Most of my businesses have been small; the most I ever had was 125 employees. More often it has been businesses with ten to fifteen employees.

When I was a boy in junior high school—they call it middle school nowadays—I had kids working for me on consignment. I've held down a lot of jobs in my life, and in most of them I was totally or virtually self-employed. When I was a salesman I sold on commission. When I drove a cab it was on "horse-hire." Instead of getting a percentage of the meter, I paid the owner of the cab a fixed number of dollars for the night. If I didn't take in that amount of dollars, I didn't just work for nothing—I paid for the privilege of working. But if I hustled, as I usually did, I made a lot more than the guys who worked on percentage. I liked it better that way. If you're the kind who prefers the percentage, keep your job. If you'd prefer horse-hire, read on. This book may be for you.

I've been an insurance broker, I've driven a beer truck, I've sold things door-to-door. I've sold ice cream from a truck in an inner city ghetto where nobody else wanted to work. I've owned a small luncheonette. When I went to college I managed the snack bar and catering service of the student union building. For more than fourteen years my former wife and I owned and operated a private school and summer camp. I've been a councilman and mayor in the community in which I currently reside.

I went back to college as an adult to pick up a degree that I knew would prove useful in business as well as socially— because people attach more weight to what you say if you have a college diploma.

I never held a job or engaged in an activity, including politics, that has not been of some assistance to me in the operation of business. They have all helped me in my radio career as well. All of your experiences make you what you are and give you an understanding of what's happening. You may be a great physicist, but unless you have a much broader background and a more eclectic experience, you probably won't make it in small business.

Even though I'm on the radio every weeknight, which would be enough to keep some people busy full-time, and I'm on television occasionally, broadcasting is only one of my current involvements. I'm also busy on weekends making personal appearances around the country. I own and operate, on an absentee basis, several enterprises, including a flower business and several media-oriented operations. In partnership with my

4

oldest son, I operated a used-car rental agency and, in conjunction with that, a service station. We just acquired two radio stations, a barber shop and a bar, and I write a column syndicated to approximately 600 newspapers around the nation.

I've learned a great deal from doing the radio program, too. I've heard mistakes that a novelist couldn't dream up and unbelievable predicaments that people have worked themselves into. I've picked up a lot of street smarts along the way from a lot of highly unofficial sources. I've got something else going for me as well; I'm insatiably curious. Wherever I am, I have to ask questions and find out as much as I can. I've had some success fielding questions on the air from all over because I've been around and seen a lot and have something to offer.

All of the material in this book is designed as practical knowledge. Many vocational curricula—keeping in mind that many college degrees are in effect vocational licenses—could be taught in half the time if much of the material were discarded. The problem is that it's impossible to tell in advance which half of the curriculum to keep and which to scuttle. The student therefore has to be exposed to many components that will never come up in his or her career. The same applies in this book. Without knowing what applies to you I'll expose you to my views and my experience; it's up to you to digest what you need and ignore what you don't.

Most existing writing on small business seems to me abstract and out of touch. Most of the material has been written by professional writers or by academics, not by business people. Most of those writers don't know their subject firsthand, so they have gathered information by asking questions and writing down answers. There's nothing dishonorable about that, of course, but often they don't know the right questions to ask and often don't know that they have been given the wrong answers. I've tried to give the right answers when I've been interviewed, but I can tell you from direct experience that most of my interviewers didn't know their subject. It takes somebody who has been there to understand small business.

While I have nothing against an occasional word of inspiration, this book isn't meant as a revival meeting in print. I'm not going to give you a spurious spiel about how you can make a million dollars with no money down and won't have to work for it. If that were the case, and I knew how to do it, I wouldn't tell you. I will try to motivate you to succeed, but oratory is not the main ingredient of this volume.

It's important, I believe, to stress the hazards of small business. A lot of effusive writing about the joys and rewards of running your own business makes it sound as if it's almost impossible to fail if you believe strongly enough. The fact is, however, that the chances of success are relatively slim.

Various statistics show that four out of five small businesses fail, most of them within the first few years of operation, and that the leading cause of failure is overoptimism in sales projections. Your odds can be somewhat better than four to one if you absorb some simple principles. There are no great mysteries in small business. It's true that many snares and pitfalls lie in the way of any business, and some of those can't even be charted. I'd like to point out some of the more obvious traps, so at least you won't fall into them.

People who go into business for themselves make a lot of mistakes. I'll tell you about the many mistakes I've made in business. I've probably made more mistakes than most people. But consider the turtle: he never gets anywhere unless he sticks his neck out. If you don't make any mistakes, you're not doing anything.

I want to tell you about how to deal with bankers, about the shortcomings and benefits of accepting credit cards, the problems engendered by leases, how to hire an accountant and squeeze your money's worth out of him, what sort of insurance you ought to have, how to keep records and why you ought to keep them. I'll try to show you how you can control your expenditures and how to deal with employees. I'll spend a lot of time on government—federal, state, and local—because I have learned how crucial government relations can be to a small business.

Some of this material seems so basic that it's difficult to understand why everybody doesn't see it. But my telephone talk show has demonstrated to me that a lot of people don't see the basics.

Let me take as an example a recent call. The woman called on behalf of her husband, a machinist, making good money but becoming unwilling to watch those pistons make one more cycle. I have no trouble understanding burnout, because I had a business of my own that was making money and doing well but which I nevertheless sold because I couldn't bear it anymore. This couple live in Minneapolis, and his plan was to go south, buy used cars there, and drive them up to Minneapolis to sell at a profit. Minneapolis people, it appears, think local used cars are not such a good buy because all the salt and chemicals thrown on the local roads during the snow-filled winters takes a toll on them. They prefer used cars from Georgia or Arizona. The idea to fill this need by shuttling cars north for sale seemed good. The problem was that he had only a $2,000 cushion to work with, and his wife was at home with a ten-month-old child.

A few minutes into the conversation I asked her if she had anyone who could baby-sit for her. She said her mother could. I asked if there were any skill she might take into the marketplace, as even some part-time work that might bring in $140 a week might make the difference. "I'm a registered nurse," she said. "I used to do private duty."

Though this man's plan had some merit, I wouldn't have given it much chance of success with only $2,000 in resources; but with a wife doing private nursing duty four times a week at $125 a shot, that's $500 in gross income per week. That should be enough to keep the wolf at least in the front yard somewhere.

You might say that any fool could have figured that out. The point, however, is that it had not occurred to them. The wife had never considered going back to work until I brought the subject up. Obviously they would have had to consider it eventually, but perhaps by then it would have been too late, since $2,000 does not last long these days. One of the commonest dilemmas of going into your own business is illustrated here—where does the sustaining income come from while you're getting started?

My Audience

Every writer—in fact every communicator—addresses himself to an audience. Some members of my own reading audience may already be in small business, and this book can be of help to them. Nevertheless I have thought of my readers as poised on the threshhold of independent enterprise.

One of them is Henry, who has been making a good living at the auto plant for the last quarter of a century. Every weekday morning he gets up very early, packs a lunch, and drives to work. All day he puts doors on the left-hand side of Chevrolets. Then he comes home, eats dinner, watches television, and drinks a six-pack of beer before going to bed. That's his life. Except that on many nights a thought steals over him as he drops off to sleep—that there must be more to life than this.

Martha graduated from Barnard College with excellent grades and a promising future. Then she met Jim and before she knew it she was married and raising a family. Now the children are out of college. Running the house is no longer a full-time job. What does she do for the rest of her life—sit in the living room and pet the dog?

For several weeks Bill has been hearing rumors about a "reduction in force." Then he received the starkest sort of confirmation—a pink slip in his pay envelope. For the last ten weeks he has been living on unemployment payments and his savings, which are beginning to get low, while looking for a job. Finding work has not been easy, and the thought of self-employment is beginning to loom on his horizon.

Murray has just graduated from college. Although ambitious and a hard worker, he has little capital to work with and has to start paying back his student loan. Ever since he was a little boy he has dreamed of having his own business. Now he's ready to begin a career—but under such stringent circumstances, can he do it?

Audrey has finished her professional studies. Now the young accountant has to decide whether to get into a public career (perhaps with the Internal Revenue Service), a private career with one of the Big Eight accounting firms, or plunge into business for herself—perhaps specializing in self-employed people.

Though still in the prime of life, Steve has accepted his company's offer to receive half-pay in exchange for early retirement. As he waits for his fifty-fifth birthday and the retirement date to arrive, he has been mulling over whether to get another job, find part-time employment, or (and this appeals especially to him) to get into a business of his own that would keep him busy six months of the year and give him the other six months off.

I complete my imaginary audience with Sam, who has already built himself a successful enterprise. Over the last decade his contracting company has flourished beyond his expectations, and he has made a considerable amount of money. After working so many years and for such long hours, tied to his local business, he has begun to regret missing out on other experiences that he once hoped for, especially the chance to travel. His children have grown, the family's financial needs have diminished, and he and his wife are willing to economize—they've already sold the house and are living year-round in their summer home. Now fifty years old, he has become tired of the responsibilities of his 150-employee company, and he wants to work on a smaller scale in a more footloose way. But he knows that the little business he has in mind has little in common with the world of big offices, secretaries, and telephones with internal switching.

All of these people, diverse though their backgrounds and their plans, are going to face some common problems. In the pages that follow I want to show you what these problems look like and the proper approaches to take.

As I discuss the problems of the businessperson, for the sake of brevity I will often use the pronoun "he." I assure you that I am well aware of the self-employed women of this country and that everything I have to say applies equally to them.

Most of what I have to impart here comes out of my own experience. I want to make it worth your dollar, and I hope that my advice will help you to succeed in whatever you commit yourself to—whether it's in a new business or a new way of looking at what you're doing now.

1

Rules of Thumb

People in business can make unique mistakes. Often, however, they make common garden-variety mistakes and have misconceptions, and here are some examples. We'll go into them in more depth, with more specifics, later.

It's More Difficult Than It Looks
This is the corollary to the commonest mistake: excessive optimism about income. "Gee," people are always saying, "I'd love to write a book. It must be glamorous to be an author." Most of them never get beyond the talking stage and so they never learn the agonies of writing.

One remark I've heard so often, since I'm in the business, is this: "I'd love to be in the flower business—it would be so cute!" There's nothing cute about the flower business. It's dirty and slimy. The battle against fungus and bugs never ends. You have to lug heavy buckets of water until your shoulders ache. Your best customer is the big, yawning dumpster out back. But people don't see that. Why? Because they're not supposed to see it. They see the pretty ribbons, somebody snipping and arranging with a tiny pair of scissors. Find out what a business is *really* like before you get into it.

13

You're Not Really Free

You must treat employees as the valuable assets they are. You must keep yourself disciplined. If you have to blow up, do it in the back room or, better yet, the backyard—never at your customers. Nobody ever won an argument with a customer. It may feel good for thirty seconds to tell somebody off. If a brief rush of euphoria is worth losing a customer forever, by all means show people how independent you are. If you do it often enough, however, you'll find your store deserted.

Some wholesalers can get away with almost anything. So can retailers, if they have no competition for one hundred miles around. But sooner or later someone will figure out how unpopular you are and will open a competing business across the street, and you may eventually become another business failure statistic.

The Money Belongs to the Business

Frequently, if you ask a businessperson how much he or she is making, you'll get the reply, "Oh, about $100,000." You then ask for clarification: "Is that gross or net? Do you *earn* that much or *gross* that much? More often than not they're talking about how much they take in. By definition, the amount of dollars that are taken in before any expenses or costs are taken into account is called gross (which means gross sales, not to be confused with gross profit). A fatal error begins here. Someone who quotes you his gross in reply to what is he making is operating on the premise that the money in the register belongs to him, and nothing could be farther from the truth.

This is particularly true when someone purchases an existing business, such as a grocery store, with inventory already in place. He finds $1,000 in the register at the end of the day. For some reason he assumes that the shelves will replenish themselves automatically without cost. Therefore the $1,000 he took in that day is his. That is the key to bankruptcy, and it's hard to believe how common it is. Soon he begins to wonder why the gross is falling off. The answer is because there isn't as much merchandise to sell. And now he hasn't as much money as before with which to replenish it. Failure feeds on failure.

The Cost of Employees Is Often Underestimated

If you agree to pay someone five dollars an hour for a 40-hour week, what are that employee's wages? If your answer is $200, you're way under the mark. In addition to the $200 base salary, you must add the cost of workers compensation. That will vary dramatically from industry to industry; in an office situation it may be rather low, but in a wood shop, where employees are using power tools that could lop off fingers and arms, the risk and the price are higher. In addition you will be required to make a contribution to your state unemployment fund, as well as a separate federal unemployment compensation contribution and Social Security payments.

Beyond this you may have agreed to provide hospitalization coverage, life insurance, and medical and dental insurance. All of these additional costs have to be added up. The likelihood is that the employee is not costing you five dollars an hour, but somewhere between six and seven dollars—the true cost of putting that employee on your payroll. When you are establishing the cost of doing business and providing the goods or services that you are in the business of providing, you must take into account *all* overhead, including the fringe benefits that your employees "enjoy."

People Assume That They Are Doing Well

One night I received a call from a Maine man who was making about $17,500 as a state employee; his wife made about $14,000, so together their income was sufficient. He wanted to quit his job and go into the insurance and securities business, which he was already doing in his spare time. He said he was doing quite well at it. He was so persuaded of it that he was ready to give up his salary, which was not princely but adequate, because he was making a lot of money at a part-time job.

I asked him how much he had made at it the previous year. About $3,000, he said. Well, that doesn't tell us much, so the next part of the equation is: How long did it take to make that $3,000? His answer was twenty hours a week.

Now let's multiply that times fifty weeks a year—we'll give him two weeks off for vacation. It comes to one thousand hours. He worked one thousand hours to make $3,000. It doesn't require a mathematics whiz to figure that his income was three dollars an hour. That's less than minimum wage. If he chose to increase his work time to sixty hours a week, that lucky soul could figure to make $9,000 a year. That's about half again as many hours as he worked at his state job, but it's much less money.

I don't believe the argument that his efficiency would increase that much by working at the job full-time. Most beginners really believe that they are doing super as they go down for the third and final gasp. You can fool your friends, and you can fool your neighbors, and your husband or wife, but there's one person you don't want ever to fool, and that's the person you're looking at when you shave or make up your face in the morning. Most of us are guilty of self-deception because we want so much to succeed.

Don't Buy a Job

If you have $200,000 at your disposal, it ought to bring you, if you invest it with some finesse—$20,000 a year in investment interest. If you have $100,000 in inventory sitting on your shelves and your business is located on real estate worth $100,000, you have given up $20,000 in investment income, because the money would have made that much for you. And if you have invested that $200,000 in an enterprise that makes you $20,000 a year, you have bought yourself a job. It's an unproductive job because you could have made as much by investing it. The principle of this is the same even if you had to borrow the money.

People do this all the time. I have people call me every night with proposals that amount to buying a job. These people could go out and make as much money working as an employee somewhere without the headaches and the sleepless nights of owning a business.

It could be argued that if you began with borrowed money and you are paying off the loan, eventually you'll start making more money for yourself. It could also be argued that certain tax advantages are gained in running a business that are not available in investing money. These are valid considerations but the rule still stands: Don't buy a job.

The Joys of Unregulation

One of my criteria for selecting a business at the present time would be to try a field with minimum governmental interference. For instance, I'd never go into the nursery school and summer camp business again—too many government agencies breathe down your neck, including boards of health, nutritional boards, the State Department of Education, the Bureau of Camper Safety, and bus transportation officials.

My wholesale flower business lies at the opposite end of the scale; there's hardly any regulation. Import restrictions are involved in shipping plants and flowers from abroad, but that's taken care of by the wholesalers with whom I deal.

Apprentice Yourself

Selecting the business you go into is of primary importance, and we will discuss it in detail at the proper moment. It's equally important, however, whatever business you choose, to see it clearly. Don't make the mistake of thinking that the cute little business down the street is a piece of cake. How do you find out? The best way is to get a job in the field. Apprentice yourself if necessary.

My ex-wife put herself through college working in a flower shop. When we decided to go into the flower business, she called her former employer's son (her employer had gone to his reward) and cut a deal whereby she would work literally for nothing for a couple of months. In return he would teach her a lot of the things she didn't know or had forgotten. She's always had a talent for arranging flowers, but there's a lot more than that to running a flower operation.

You should be absolutely up front with the owner about what you are doing. Tell him that you're willing to work hard at a modest rate of pay so that you can learn from him. Tell him that you'd like to pick his brains and you'd appreciate pointers. You can tell him on your word of honor that you won't become his competitor; you don't intend to open a place down the street but in another trade area.

I have a friend in landscaping who maintains that he put three-quarters of the landscapers in the area into business. They came to him either out of high school or college, worked for him a few years, learned the business, and then struck out for themselves. He has no objection to that, because he gets a good tradeoff. He gets a superior worker, although for a relatively short period of time, and doesn't have to pay as much as he otherwise might.

Look for someone who enjoys the role of a mentor. Most people who are good at their craft want to pass their accumulated wisdom on to someone else. And if you work at a trade for a while and discover that it's no place for you, isn't that less expensive than learning it with your own company? The surface appearance of a business is seldom what it's really like. In order to understand tailoring, you've got to see the seams of the coat.

Set Your Target from the Start

There's a barber in my town who cuts hair by appointment only. You can enter his place and find him sitting there reading the newspaper, but he won't cut your hair. He's after the appointment trade. Just as the barber has decided upon his market, you have to do the same. It may be the most important decision you make. Cut yourself a share of the market; don't try to be all things to all people.

You can't go high-end and low-end at the same time. You can't be Fast-Food Charlie's and Le Château Vieux at the same time. There's something to be said for each kind of place, but there are a lot more Charlies, because a lot more people can afford them. I like the low-end, high-volume side. My father told me, and I think he was right, that a fast nickel is better than a slow dime. Other people want to work the high-end side, and that's fine.

Having *no* target is like the football coach who gets to the stadium with the idea that he'll see how the other team plays before he works out any plays of his own. You may have to reverse yourself after you go into business because you misconceived your target, but reversal is far better than no game plan at all.

Know Thyself

When you go into your own business, you have to become a generalist. You can't afford a staff of thirty experts, each working on a specialty. You do just about everything until you get big enough to do otherwise. If you have a service station and you don't like to change oil, you have to do it anyway.

If, however, you don't have any talent for doing your tax return, that's quite another matter. Have someone else do it. Know your weaknesses and overcome them by getting others to do what you can't do well.

One of my own weaknesses is record-keeping. I'd rather clean a septic tank with my fingers than do two hours of paperwork. I'm no good at it, anyway. I hire other people to do much of it for me, and I'll tell you about that later.

A more complicated weakness is that I am not a good negotiator. Some people love it; possibly they lived previous lives in

India, where haggling is a national pastime. I know a million-aire who goes to buy his cars at a huge auto dealership in Pennsylvania where haggling is the main attraction. I find it uncomfortable to buy a car because I figure that the next person who walks in is going to get the same car for less.

In my wholesale business, I set prices and I stick to them. None of my customers will ever find that one is getting a better deal than another. I operate on the premise that most people secretly don't like haggling over prices. Nevertheless this shortcoming has hurt me at times in my businesses. When I get into a situation in which negotiation figures importantly, I hire somebody to handle that part of the enterprise for me. For example, I use an agent to negotiate my media contracts.

Ask the Boss

Being an employee has its advantages, and just because you own the business does not mean you have to give up all of those benefits. Although your ego wants to shout that the place belongs to you, it may sometimes be to your advantage to give the impression that you are an employee. My son Matthew, who was my partner in our car rental and service station business, seldom admitted that he was the boss. It saved him a lot of hassles. If someone walked in with a problem—some imperfection in the performance of a rented car, for example—Matthew would talk with the customer and they would agree that one day subtracted from the rental cost was fair compensation for the imperfection. He would offer to take the matter up with the boss (who was never in) and see what he could get for the customer. The customer got the free day, but he got it from a nice young man who stuck his neck out, not from the difficult (always absentee) boss.

Not being the boss also helped him get a mortgage for a house. On applying to the bank he listed his income but did not mention that he was half-owner of the business from which the

20

income came. The income level satisfied the bank, but had he indicated that he was self-employed it would have been questioned, and he would have had to file financial statements. It is easier to get a loan as an employee than as a self-employed person.

The Risks Are Yours

There's nothing wrong with being an employee. Some people like to have jobs that give them the leisure to do the things that really interest them. They trade some of their time for money and leave space for being with their sweethearts or their children, going to football games, swapping jokes at the corner tavern, civic duties in the League of Women Voters, visiting antique stores—whatever interests and absorbs them.

Some people like the security of a job. Life is difficult enough without the additional perils of self-employment. There's nothing more inhibiting for some people than the terrifying thought that if they were to quit the job and go into business for themselves, there would be no regular weekly paycheck.

Some people are skittish about being in business for themselves. They like the idea of independence, but they're not certain that they have the business mentality. Their doubt gives evidence of their good sense, because they probably would not succeed in the entrepreneurial mode.

Some people just seem born to be employees. I know one of these who runs the business for his boss, a man who has vision problems and never comes to work anymore. This fellow could buy a business and run it himself. He does it now. He hires, he fires, he takes care of the money, he opens, closes, answers the telephone, books appointments. But he won't leave; he likes working for his boss. "I don't want the headaches of my own business," he said. Actually he has all the headaches already. He's the perfect employee. Most people are employees. But they're not as perfect as this one.

Some people are not self-starters. They need somebody to tell them to get to work on time, and they have enough self-awareness to know it.

These kinds of people are employees. The world needs them. One of the rewards they get from being an employee is letting someone else take the risks.

For the entrepreneur, however, one of the major pleasures is taking the risks himself. The entrepreneur finds more fun in that than in leisure.

Why? Because the entrepreneur is hungry. That doesn't really answer anything, though. Being hungry doesn't have anything to do with being poor. Admittedly, if you don't have money, that's an additional incentive. But for most of the hungry people—that's the original Mellons, Fords, Rockefellers, and Carnegies who made the fortunes—money was not what they worked for. Up to a point, money is a barometer of success, but not a goal.

One day recently I was listening to the radio—to a talk show, as usual. The hostess was asking people what they would do if they were to become a big-money lottery winner. How would that change your life? That brought a lot of calls. As I listened I thought: Would it change my life? I'd still go to work every day. I'd continue doing my radio show. I'd stay involved in my little business enterprises. As ever, I'd be working ten or twelve hours a day. It's clear that money isn't the only thing that motivates me.

Most of the people I know in their own business who are really successful are like me—always planning the next move. At three o'clock in the morning, sometimes, they're unable to sleep. I have a successful friend who often gets up at 4 A.M. and drives to the office. He has a problem he wants to attack and becomes restless.

The Business Comes First
Many people believe that self-employment offers a time flexi-

bility that is impossible for an employee. There is probably some truth to that in a mature enterprise. It is absolutely not the case, however, in the formative years of an enterprise, during which you become a virtual slave to your business.

"I thought that I'd be working less in my own business," one of my callers told me. "I thought I'd be the boss and set my own hours." You'll set your own hours, all right, but you'll undoubtedly set them higher. People who operate their own businesses, by and large, work the hardest of anybody in our society—and have to take more care that their leisure time doesn't interfere with work. "When I worked at the agency," one professional told me, "I could stay up half the night drinking and carousing. I don't do it anymore. If I'm coasting along in the morning nursing a hangover, it's on my own time, not on my boss's time."

I've often told my kids that I've never regarded myself as a whole lot brighter than the next person. (Well, maybe a little.) The edge I've had over other people throughout most of my life has been my ability and my willingness to work sixteen or seventeen hours a day. If you are not ready to do that, there is no serious business for you to get into.

You may not see much of your family. I've always been able to steal a couple of hours to see my sons play football or my daughters basketball. That's because my businesses have usually been only a short sprint from home. Not every entrepreneur has that opportunity. Through most of my careers the hours have been unbelievably long. When one of my sons was small, he was playing with a friend who told him: "My daddy had to work overtime."

"What's overtime?" my son asked.

"That means he had to work on Saturday."

"Saturday?" my son repeated, puzzled. "Doesn't everybody work Saturday?"

For years we made no distinction between day and night, weekdays and weekends; it was all work time. The business

23

always came first. The family had to do without things so that the money could be socked back into the business. For two years we all but abolished Christmas presents.

In the early 1960s we put down a deposit on a summer home at the New Jersey shore. We were running a day camp at that time, and swimming pools were becoming a standard facility at camps. Unquestionably, to remain competitive we had to have such a pool, and we just could not afford that and the summer home as well. I had to ask for, and was decently given, my deposit back. That might be a flawed example of sacrifice, because our kids loved the pool at the camp and used it all the time. I, however, had wanted the summer home much more.

For years, while we operated the nursery school and camp, we used the school bus as our family car. For two years we slept on a mattress on the floor because we couldn't spend the money for a bed. We did not own a television set for several years because we could not afford one. All our money was being reinvested in the business. Our children had to learn that they did not get what other kids got, did not get to do what other kids got to do.

The self-employed businessperson is not just willing to work hard, but also to sacrifice immediate pleasures for the long view. Many talented people who like absorbing work, who find adventure in their careers, and who have their egos committed to success are nonetheless unable to postpone their gratification. They want those perks and that boat. That's perfectly okay, but they are not quite cut out for working for themselves. When they go into business for themselves they often buy things for themselves that they do not need because personal gratification is highly important to them. That kind of buying, incidentally, is another leading cause of business failures.

The older you get, the more you are likely to find physical limitations beginning to creep into the hard and demanding work of the entrepreneur. At sixty years of age, you may not be able to put in the long hours that the work requires. By that age, however, you should have picked up some savvy along the way. Like the pitcher who can't throw the blazing fastball anymore but has become smarter, the older entrepreneur has some compensating experience to make up for the flagging of stamina. Still, even in their sixties and seventies the entrepreneur outworks others his own age.

Eventually, it is hoped, the entrepreneur is compensated for all the years he or she has been nurturing the business.

When you look at some of the outstanding properties in resort areas—amid the ski trails or along the coastline—and you ask who owns that big place, you'll usually hear something to the effect that it's Mr. Potter, who owns Potter Electronics. And the big one a little farther down the road? That one belongs to Mr. Fulsome of Fulsome Chemicals. You'll rarely hear that it's Mr. McNeill, an executive with Potter Electronics or with Fulsome Chemicals. The people who are making the big money in the United States are the people who own their own enterprises. Many more people are making a half-million dollars a year in "small business" than are top corporate executives in "big business."

The Problems of Part-time Entrepreneurs

Many regularly employed people supplement their income with part-time enterprises of their own. Such enterprises often work out for people with what might be called the car-pool kind of job (which begins and ends at the same time every day), or people with unusual work schedules, such as airline pilots, who usually lay over several days between flights.

Part-time enterprises that are operated by appointment only can often be arranged so as not to interfere with full-time employment. Most real estate, for example, is sold in the evening or on weekends, easily slotted into a schedule for a person who works days. Some mechanics even repair automobiles at night, by appointment. Some tavernkeepers operate their bars only at night as a subsidiary occupation, but that's a big-city phenomenon; in small towns where liquor licenses are rare and much coveted, the license is too valuable to let the place sit idle during the day.

Although it sounds good, part-time supplementary work often does not live up to expectations. Wherever rental costs are high, part-time enterprises that rent space are probably unfeasible. Many people have taken up night-hour cleaning services as a dandy second job only to find that so much physical effort at day's end, after a full day's work, has them staggering and falling into the pail.

I don't encourage people to go into entrepreneurial ventures on a part-time basis. Many people apparently believe it would be easy to hold down a salaried job and build a little independent business on the side. They forget that their competition will be working full-time.

Granted that you can maintain a part-time business on a low-gear level. Your cellar is your office; you need no employees because you can persuade your spouse or press your children into service; as for insurance, you just don't carry it; and burning the midnight lamps only hikes the electric bill a little. You can get away with that, as long as the business chugs along on the hobby level.

If you are committing real money to your venture, however, you want every edge possible. What happens when your boss calls upon you to stay late, and you have another commitment that evening? Then you have a heavy decision to make. And what will the decision be? If you have any sense, you will favor your major source of income over your minor source. That does not bode well for your little part-time business.

Let's say that you have a vending-machine route, which you work evenings, and you have a salaried job during the day. You get a call from one of your major plants that the machines have run out of everything. The manager who calls you does not care that you are sitting at a desk ten miles away at your salaried job. What do you mean, he says, you can't get here until nine o'clock? He put in these vending machines to keep his workers happy. And he has two shifts coming and going before nine o'clock. What do you do then? (And don't delude yourself that this will never happen; it will probably happen once a week.)

"I'm going to start part-time at first so I can keep my job." That's probably what the fellow said when he halfheartedly entered the vending-machine business. That's often the ticket to failure. The current estimate of failed businesses is 400,000 annually in the United States. These businesses failed for a lot of different reasons, but let me point out one that is seldom mentioned—lack of commitment. They failed because the going became rough, and the part-time business was exposed for what it really was—a hobby.

That's what's wrong with part-time jobs. They're too easy to quit. In fact, if the full-time job is placed in jeopardy, that's often what happens. If there is a back door to walk out of, most people will walk out of it. That's only human. In any enterprise, you keep an eye on the back door, ready to bail out. When you become fed up with frustrations, and nothing goes right, and everything is falling in on you, that back door tempts you to distraction. But if there is no back door—if this is your only career—you have to stand where you are and deal with whatever comes. So often that makes the difference between making it or failing—making it because you have to make it.

Are You Kidding?

I am always getting calls from people with "a great idea." America, it seems, is swarming with "great ideas." A typical caller will tell me that he has come up with the greatest thing since the zipper. How, he then asks, does a little fellow like himself go about interesting a big company in buying or subsidizing this great idea? I ask him why he needs to have a big company back him. Because, he says, this idea is going to take some development money. I ask him: Do you have a source of money you can call upon? For example, how about selling your house and putting the money into the project? The reaction to that often raises the sound level. "Sell my house!" the caller says, recoiling in dismay. "Are you kidding? I can't sell my house! It's all we've got!"

Taking a gut-wrenching risk is too much for some people, which is often what stands between them and success. Our greatest resource is not our houses but our own personal inner resources, such as what our grandparents called pluck—that is, a kind of quiet, low-level courage. What the sputtering caller is telling me with his response is that his great idea has been overestimated. It's not really such a great idea after all. It isn't worth any real risks to its creator. If you lack the confidence to back your idea with your house, what chance does that idea have? The man or woman willing to back the idea with the family jewels—that's the one who has a chance. Those people, however, constitute a small minority. What makes success is not a "great idea"—which has limited value as long as it remains only an idea—but someone with the courage to see the idea through to execution. To paraphrase the caller, the question is: Are you kidding? Or are you serious?

2

Getting Started

I started hustling at an early age; I was working regularly on a six-days-a-week basis at twelve years old. I worked at a market, making deliveries, cutting meat, cleaning up, anything, for six dollars a week. I had to work, if I wanted any money. My family had been well-do-do, but the business went to hell during the Depression.

At Christmastime I'd go out into the woods to cut down birch trees—needless to say, unbeknownst to the owners—from which I would make Yule logs, putting candles on them and selling them door-to-door. I also went to a supplier and bought Christmas corsages, at eighteen cents each, and mistletoe by the box at a cheap rate because the berries were falling off. I'd get cellophane bags, drop a sprig of mistletoe into each bag, throw in some loose berries, so it all looked like one piece, and then sell the mistletoe to people on the basis that this way, cased in cellophane, the berries wouldn't stain the rug or poison the kids or the dog. I took stuff that would ordinarily be thrown away and sold it at a premium.

My best friend and I would rent a store right across the street from a big elementary school, and we'd hire kids, on consignment, to sell the corsages and the mistletoe door-to-door. We'd have as many as four hundred kids on any given day fanned out across a whole section of the city. We made money on everything they sold.

It got so that people used to tack a piece of mistletoe onto the door to keep the kids away, as a sign that they had already bought the stuff. Then we'd move on to the next school. We made more money at Christmas than most youngsters made all year long.

IMPORTANT CONSIDERATIONS

Two Types of Businessperson

Are you a Type One businessperson, or a Type Two?

Type One is the sort of person who starts a business from scratch. He sees a vacuum and rushes to fill it. He is an original. The prototype of this sort was Juan Trippe, who founded Pan American Airlines in the 1920s, flying tourists to Cuba and establishing the first regularly scheduled passenger air service. Often when a company gets bigger and bigger the Type One businessperson may lose control of it, as Trippe did with Pan Am, and Steven Jobs with Apple computers.

Type Two is a bean counter, the detail-oriented sort. He's a manager, carries a table of organization in his head, and is the first person to sense that one of the company's divisions needs an additional unit. He's growth-oriented. He would probably be a complete loss, however, at trying to start an enterprise from nothing because he needs the material, the charts and figures, to work with.

The Type Two sort always heads for the mail first thing and sorts it out by category. The Type One person shovels the mail into a bag and promises to go through it next week. Type One, however, can take the same bag into the bank with him and walk out with a bagful of money. He is probably a salesman by temperament, although not always by practice or profession.

I'm a start-up sort myself, not an expander. Businesses, because I tend eventually to become bored with them, have a way of outgrowing me. It's rare that a person combines the qualities of Type One and Type Two. Are you the sort of person who ought to build a new enterprise? Or the sort who should take over an existing enterprise? There ought to be litmus paper you would lick to find out; if it turns pink you go one way, if it turns blue the other.

In the absence of such a test, it's important that you ask yourself some questions about which type you are. Are you more detail-oriented? Are you more security-oriented? You're probably a Type Two. Can you cope with not having money come in every week? If you can't, you're a Type Two personality. Do you bore easily? You're probably a Type One.

The Type Two person keeps regular hours; the Type One person is liable to be found at the office at 3 A.M. It's also possible he may be found in bed at 10 A.M. The Type One person is more erratic, more likely to do things when it strikes him. Type One doesn't manage time as well as Type Two, because Type One probably doesn't think in terms of time.

Type Two individuals can do extremely well in their own businesses, but they probably ought to take over an existing business rather than start a new one. A Type Two person may not be able to handle days during which not a single customer walks through the door.

Renting Versus Owning

Most of the experts tell us that renting is the better way to operate a business. The prevailing theory is that you are not in the real estate business, but in the beer business or the widget business or whatever, and your efforts and capital should be concentrated on beer, or widgets, and not on real estate.

Renting gives you tax advantages because the rent can be written off as a straight expense. You cannot write off the property you own that easily; you have to depreciate it over a period of time. A purchased piece of heavy equipment must be depreciated over a specified period, and the Internal Revenue Service may dispute your rate of depreciation. This is one of the reasons why contractors often sell their heavy equipment to a bank and then lease it back. It's all done on paper, of course, and the equipment never actually leaves the yard. Sometimes a company will build a plant to its own specifications, then sell the building and lease it back. It gives the company just what it is looking for, but keeps its money free to use in developing its business.

When you depreciate property, you may have to defend your accounting before the IRS. You may contend that the property completely depreciates in three years; the government may contend that you should depreciate it over a decade. The difference of opinion centers about the useful life of the equipment.

When an individual rents a piece of equipment, a building, or anything else, the investment and the indebtedness (and that's the operative word here) does not show up on the balance sheet as a liability. If you borrowed money to purchase the equipment, however, it does show up as a liability. The latter can create problems for you.

For example, if you go to a bank to borrow money for some purchase (let's say for replenishing inventory), the bank may say that you appear to be fairly deeply in hock already and that you cannot afford to get any deeper. Therefore the bank may turn down your loan request or charge you a higher interest rate. If you bid for any work that requires a performance bond, the bonding company may take a similar attitude—it may feel that you are carrying too many liabilities to bond you, or it may want to charge you a higher premium. (A performance bond is put up by an outside company as a guarantee that you will perform the work, or the company will pay for any losses involved in your failure to perform it.) On the other hand, your rental costs don't create such situations for you.

In some businesses you don't have the choice of owning versus renting. In large malls, for example, owning is out of the question. A few condominium malls are in operation, but they are rare, and malls, which are so important to the retailing of our time, are almost totally a rental environment. If you want to set up a nut shop in one of those freestanding kiosks in a mall, you have to rent.

On the other hand, owning has its advantages too. One of them is the opportunity to depreciate. I'm not going all that deeply into the subject, since depreciation laws and IRS rules keep changing all the time. In effect there are two ways of depreciating—straight-line or accelerated—and the way you depreciate should be chosen after consulting with a knowledgeable accountant who can advise you as to which is more to your advantage.

A second tax advantage in owning is that any interest you pay to the bank (or for that matter to any mortgage holder) for your mortgage is tax deductible.

An additional advantage: in an inflationary economy such as ours has been (and, judging from the budget deficits of the period, will probably continue to be) property tends to keep pace. Depending on its location, real property sometimes outpaces inflation. Buying property is a risk, nevertheless, because if you buy in the wrong place or events take an adverse turn—if the base of the town's economy shuts down for good, for example—your property values may take a beating.

Personally, I like to own the ground under my feet. On several occasions, however, I have rented property, started a business there, and subsequently purchased the property. I rented with an option to buy, which costs a little more but hedges your bet. If the site turns out to be wrong, you can pack up and leave without complications.

Locating Your Business
If you're starting up a new business, where to put it?

Remember that high visibility—a first-floor location in an attractive and busy commercial area—is going to cost more money. Is this high visibility necessary? If you're a retailer selling to the public, it usually helps. Your location is a form of advertising. They may not be interested in selling their gold chains today but if they walk past a store that bears a sign "We Buy Gold Chains" often enough, they may think of your place when the question of selling comes up.

On the other hand, if you're selling pocketbook liners, you're not dealing with the public, but with the trade; the trade will find you. You don't have to be in the high-rent district. In a major city you may want to be in the district where that kind of commerce, in this case pocketbook manufacture, is carried on. You can be on the fifth floor, in the back of the building, with an encoded message on the door, and the trade will find you.

There are some exceptions to the rule that retailing ought to be done in highly visible places.

New York is one of the top high-rent areas of the world. One store well-known for photographic and recording equipment has maintained a second-floor operation for many years. If you didn't know the location of the store you would be unlikely to walk up that narrow flight of stairs in that nondescript building for fear you might get mugged. When you get up the stairs, though, you'll find crowds standing eight deep to be waited on. The reason: the store advertises heavily and sells at discount. The owners have taken a high-traffic location in Manhattan, but not a high-visibility location. If the store were moved down to the first floor its rent would probably quadruple. The owners have made a business decision to price low and advertise heavily rather than pay high rents. It has worked for this store for a long time—so successfully that the company has opened a second store in a similar location one block away.

Some businesses are indifferent about walk-in business, or want to discourage it. A highly specialized consulting firm has no need to be accessible to the public. Some insurance brokers never see clients in their offices, but always go to them. A company that deals exclusively in door-to-door selling needs no high-rent district location.

Leases

You've built a great business and you want to sell it; you look at your lease and it says you can't transfer the lease. You can't sell it. A lease is a two-edged sword; remember that before you get into it.

The lease has its advantages. You can't be summarily kicked out. Landlords as a class aren't stupid. If your landlord watches your ice-cream parlor turn into a huge success and you have a one-year lease, he may decide not to renew it, and go into the business himself. So in that sense you have some protection with a longer lease.

But do you want to sign a ten-year lease? If it's for $1,000 a month, you've committed yourself to $120,000. The enormity of it staggers, and here you should certainly have a lawyer at work, looking for the little one-liners that can sink the *Titanic*. Anyone who signs a standard landlord's lease for a commercial property without having a lawyer look at it ought to have his head examined. It gives the landlord everything except rights to your spouse; that's why it's called a landlord's lease.

When you take it to your attorney he will cross out paragraphs 27, 32, 34, and 44 and add paragraphs 73, 74, and 75. He will explain the implications of these clauses to you—the paragraph, for example, that makes you responsible for any improvements required by any government agency. That means a sprinkler system, a fallout shelter, or whatever the government demands.

A lease means you cannot move into larger quarters if your business takes off. It may mean that you are stuck in a shopping center after the anchor store (the big department store) has gone out of business and the place has become a ghost town. There is nothing in the lease to protect you, and the center owner, believe me, has other problems to contend with.

In many cases when you get a lease, all you get in the allotted space is the partitions. The rest is up to you. And in some cases you have to leave it behind when you leave—not counters or refrigerators, but improvements to the interior.

Often you can negotiate within a lease. Suppose you're negotiating a three-year lease. You have confidence in your business and you're sure it will prosper, but what if the unexpected happens, and you're sitting there with a lease with two years left to run. While negotiating you can write in a buy-out clause—perhaps expressed in terms of three months' rent. By paying it you can get out of the lease. However, if you're looking for an escape hatch, the landlord will probably want the same. If he gets the same thing, he can buy you out by letting you have three months' free rent—and then put his brother-in-law in the successful ice-cream business that you started.

In most shopping centers, signing a lease brings on a host of other obligations. Some people don't realize that *in addition to* the rent, they will be assessed for a share of the local property taxes, billed for their share of the costs of plowing that huge parking lot when it snows, billed for cleaning the lot and perhaps for private security guards. And if you make over a certain amount in a month the mall may be entitled to a percentage of the excess because, after all, you're making money so they should be making some of it, too.

This may be important to check if you run a sale. Suppose you're selling some goods at a loss just to move them out, and you thereby attract a lot of additional business. The mall takes a part of that, even though you're losing money. So maybe instead of running a sale you ought to take the goods to a liquidator. Maybe you should—but maybe according to the mall contract you can't.

Malls are rarely negotiable for the little business. You get the standard contract, take it or leave it. If you do find that you have some leverage, it probably means the mall is doing poorly.

PURCHASING AN ESTABLISHED BUSINESS

Why Is the Business for Sale?

One of the first questions that must be addressed when you're buying a business is, Why is the present owner selling it?

Be advised that the answer you get is not always the real reason. Often as not it's horsefeathers. Frequently the real reason is perfectly acceptable and would not discourage a knowledgeable buyer. Many an owner, however, has persuaded himself that his interests are better served by concocting an excuse for selling.

One of the true reasons is often: "I'm fed up with it. I've had it." The owner doesn't wish to admit that he's reached his limits, that he's over his head. Burnout is an excellent reason to sell a business, maybe the best reason of all. It occurs in every enterprise; it is particularly prevalent when a Type One individual who has founded the business has run the course. Often, however, the burned-out entrepreneur will invent some other reason to cushion his ego. When burnout occurs, the business often starts to slip, and that is difficult to admit.

I can tell you that from personal experience. The first time it happened it almost destroyed me. "What the hell is this?" I thought. "I can't run my own business." The second time it happened it was easier to face.

Sometimes a death has occurred in the business, taking either the owner or a key figure in the enterprise. The surviving members of the enterprise may be incapable of or may lack interest in keeping the operation going.

Often an owner has overextended himself—he has more than one enterprise and has to sell one to save the other. On the other hand, he may be selling because he knows that a competitor is about to open around the corner. This should not discourage you—competition can be positive—but it may force operational changes that the current owner is unwilling or unable to make.

Buying from a burned-out entrepreneur is often a good deal. He or she wants to get out and thus is willing to carry some of your paper (help finance your purchase). You can walk into the deal with less cash and more credit.

Being Smaller Helps

It has become common for supermarket chains to sell off individual stores. What can be a losing proposition for a big chain may be turned around when the owner manages the store on the premises. He doesn't carry all the heavy overhead of the big organization. He can not only manage the store but can also double as his own produce manager or his own deli manager, or both. With an owner on the premises, an additional benefit is that shrinkage will decrease and efficiency increase. (Shrinkage in this case means goods that never reach the checkout counter for a variety of reasons, including theft, spoilage, and breakage.)

The big organization, with heavier administration problems, needs submanagers, regional managers who oversee a group of store managers, and a manager who oversees the regional managers.

While you should look with a grain of skepticism at the notion that you can make a go of it when the previous owner could not, you may be right. Not just because you're young, ambitious, and destined to succeed, but because you are looking at the operation with fresh eyes. If you've ever moved out of a house or an apartment, you may remember what a revelation it can be. "I never realized," you'll say to yourself, "how badly this room needed a paint job." The new entrepreneur walking in sees the need for sprucing up, refurbishing, repairing—and may therefore do better at the same location.

How Much Is It Worth?

One of the major problems to face anyone buying a business is how to get at the truth about its worth. It won't surprise the IRS, I'm sure, to read here that the typical entrepreneur has been spending the last fifteen years trying to take money out of the business, keep book profits down, invent various expenses, and in some cases just skim by dealing in cash. This has been to his advantage over the years.

It is not to his advantage, however, when the time comes to sell the place. The buyer asks to see his income tax returns and is told, "What income tax? I haven't paid any income tax in thirty years." (The same problem occurs when the small businessperson applies for a bank loan; if he's never claimed more than $9,000 in income over the last twenty years, it's hard to go to a bank and borrow money on his thriving enterprise.)

One of the best ways to solve this dilemma is to get the seller to agree to a deal—tying the sales price to a guaranteed gross income over a period of years. Instead of relying either on the owner's books (a fictional tale of hand-to-mouth existence) or on his promises of incredible riches out of the Arabian Nights, base it on verifiable performance.

Let's say you've agreed on a $40,000 purchase price payable over a three-year period, with one-quarter down. He assures you that the business will gross $100,000 per year. You pay $10,000 down (25 percent). The second $10,000 payment is due at the end of the first year—but only if the operation in fact grosses $100,000. If it only grosses $90,000, you pay only $9,000, and if it only grosses $80,000, you pay only $8,000. The same agreement would hold for the second- and third-year payments. A clause could also be written in—the seller might suggest it—that a sweetener be thrown into your payments if the business does *better* than $100,000 per year. You would also probably have to guarantee quality standards equal to those of the previous owner—in maintenance, merchandise, and so forth, so as not to

39

change the character of the business. (Gross income works better for this kind of agreement than net income, since you may be following your predecessor's lead in reducing your net.)

If your agreement stretches over more than a couple of years, you also ought to have a clause in the agreement that accounts for inflation. A gross income will creep upward with inflation without producing more real income. An escalator should be built in, tied to an indicator—I prefer the treasury bill rate to the Consumer Price Index. Deflation should be addressed as well, in the unlikely event that it should occur.

That former owner may want to audit your sales so that you don't use the same methods on him that he used on the government. The wary seller will insist upon, and is entitled to, reasonable controls to be certain that the reported gross is an accurate reflection of the business.

The world overflows with formulas about how to appraise a business, yet much of its actual value depends on what you are buying. Are you chiefly buying a location? Are you buying "good will"? Or inventory?

Inventory purchases can often tell you a lot about the worth of a business. If the owner bought goods, something must have happened to those goods. The IRS, operating on that principle, uses purchases extensively when it examines a business. Even here, however, evasions are possible. A grocery store, for example, keeps four kinds of bread in stock; three show up on the books and the fourth is always paid in cash and is unrecorded.

Be careful about buying inventory. You can expect that the seller is not going to undervalue his inventory; it's up to you to decide whether his figure rings true. He may own 5,000 wide, flowered ties, perfectly clean and well-pressed, but nobody is buying such ties right now; narrow, subdued ties are in vogue. You can't sell plastic flowers these days, especially older ones, even if they were purchased at the price your seller claims. Don't let him sell you stuff that Noah left behind when he built the

Ark, or goods that he bought from *his* predecessor, like coal-oil lamps. (Not much call for them nowadays.)

A personal aside: Although I didn't buy them as inventory, I put myself in the same kind of bind early in the flower business when, against excellent advice, I bought trivets. I bought more trivets than somebody would need to go into the trivet business. Then I spent the next few years trying to get rid of them. I took them to flea markets, gave them away as gifts, marked the price down; everything, in short, but hanging out in alleys and saying, "Hey buddy, want to buy a trivet?" I still have a lot of them. (A trivet is a short-legged, three-legged metal insulating tray, sometimes with a tile inlay.)

The value of Good Will (or, as they call it in some places, Blue Sky) is even more difficult to price. If the present owner has spent eight years establishing himself as the highest-quality, lowest-priced place for counties around, this Good Will is clearly worth something. This reputation was not established over a weekend. The customers know that the item or line of items for sale there is inexpensive, dependable, and always in stock, and will come from miles around to get it. That's what he's selling and that's what you're buying. You are paying for the time that he took to establish that reputation. As to how much it's worth—that's difficult to determine. Customer lists and mailing lists, if they exist, are included in Good Will.

An accountant may help in analyzing a business. If the present owner shows evasiveness in any area, you should exercise caution in going any farther into the agreement. The main thing to remember is that when you buy an established business you are buying instant cash, instant turnover, and that's worth something.

Restrictive Covenants

The purchase of a business can and often does include a binding guarantee that the previous owner will not open a competing business within a certain area. That can be important, because if he's a barber, for example, he can move down the street and take most of his customers with him. That means you bought the Good Will and he took the Good Will with him. Depending on the nature of the product or service, the appropriate geographical area to exclude might be two miles or might be all the territory east of the Mississippi. The restriction is enforceable if it is reasonable, and the courts have upheld that. If your covenant states that the previous owner can't open another pizza parlor in the state of Tennessee, that's probably unreasonable and unenforceable; but if it's a machine parts business, the whole of Tennessee may be a perfectly reasonable area for a restrictive covenant. It's essential that the restrictive covenant be written by an attorney who is familiar with the field.

The buyer may be reluctant to ask for a restrictive covenant, particularly if he or she is getting good terms. Actually you should not be without it. The previous owner may swear he'll never have anything to do with the business again, and mean it at the time; but six months later, bored to madness, he may plunge back in. Remember that a reasonable covenant is best, because it is enforceable and offers no escape to the seller. Don't be greedy.

And Don't Overlook These

Some other considerations that should be examined in the purchase of an established business:

Employees. Are key employees leaving the business upon transfer? Do you want to keep the present employees? Are any contracts, including union contracts, involved?

Equipment. This includes furniture and fixtures. What is their market value? How much has the present owner spent in recent years on upkeep and repairs?

Accounts receivable. Are you buying the establishment's unpaid billing, commonly called receivables? If so, are they reasonably collectable? (A bill long outstanding should be highly discounted.) Do the customers of this business tend to pay slowly? (If so, you may strain your working capital while you wait for your money.)

Accounts payable. Are you accepting responsibility for bills that the business owes? If so, they should be itemized, and an indemnification entered into against any other liabilities that are not on the itemized list.

Sometimes, incidentally, that's impossible. If you take over a corporation and hidden liabilities show up later, it's your problem. With a small corporation, you are better off to dissolve the corporation and form a new one with a similar name, or have the old corporation license your corporation to do business under the original corporate name. Thus you don't take over the corporate liabilities.

Suppliers. What kind of business relations does the present owner have with suppliers? Is the business committed to suppliers through long-standing contracts? Can you expect similar terms? Are future deliveries already ordered?

Final Steps

You may have come this far without a lawyer, but from this point you need one, especially in examining the lease or property transfer.

If a lease is being offered, your lawyer must determine whether it is transferable and whether you will enjoy identical terms from the landlord as has the present operator. You should also determine rules about changing the layout of the building's interior or exterior.

A good, long lease is a salable commodity. Sometimes, if location is paramount, it is the most important thing you buy.

I received a call from a fellow in Texas who wanted to sell his business. He operated a Christmas store that was only open two months of the year. What, I asked him, did he do with his property for the other ten months? He said he didn't have a property but just rented a new place every year. This fellow was trying to sell a business, but actually he had nothing to sell. He was little more than an itinerant peddler. Why would anyone need to buy a business from him? You could start your own business on exactly the same terms. A business with only one year to run on the existing lease is also not selling much, if it's a business in which location is an important ingredient.

If the business owner is selling a building rather than a lease, by all means you need a lawyer for what is actually a real estate transaction as well as a business purchase. The same goes for any sale in which a transfer of license is involved. Be aware of regulatory restrictions that apply to some licenses.

The liabilities of the business should be nailed down in the contract—unpaid forthcoming bills, mortgages, agreements, back taxes, liens, overdue employee benefits, pending suits. Your lawyer should include a statement that the seller assumes any undisclosed claim.

Agreement must be reached as to when the purchaser takes over the business, how the insurance coverage and taxes are to be prorated, and who will pay the legal fees.

It may be necessary to set up some escrow arrangement to handle the transition. The escrow agent—often although not necessarily a bank or attorney—serves as an interim arrangement during the conveyance of the business until all conditions on both sides are met.

STARTING YOUR OWN BUSINESS

Starting a new business of your own is even more difficult than buying an established business, for it has no momentum and no cash flow. Presumably you have some prior experience in the field, have been doing it in your off-hours, or are planning to begin it as a part-time operation and shift into full-time later. Here are some tips that apply to your situation, and may apply to taking over an established business as well.

Floor Layout

Designing a floor layout for a business operation can be maddeningly difficult. The kitchen area of a restaurant, for example, can be full of access problems and space problems that never occurred to you until you began to try to place the sinks, the refrigerator, and the swinging doors.

Nevertheless, whatever your field, you can find counterparts to your business in the area. Drop in on businesses similar to your own. Pace out your competitors. Tally up their floor space. If you are going to have a card shop, count the number of card gondolas that your competitors have. They have been around for a while and are trying to maximize business in the same way that you intend. Look at their decorating materials. Owners who have been in business for some time have undoubtedly redecorated. They made mistakes the first time—they bought a tile that collected dirt or a rug that wore quickly—and they learned by those mistakes. So copy them. Why come up with your own ideas when you can easily borrow someone else's?

What I find useful is to make a scale model of the store or work area involved, and then cut counters, gondolas, display racks, and so forth to scale and move them around. It's surprising how much you can learn from this exercise, and you can frequently see where an error might have been made. It is much less expensive and easier to do this than it is to have things custom made and then find out for whatever reason that they don't work, or there was a better way. The viability of this approach can be demonstrated easily when examining new buildings. Architects almost universally have a model made of the building before the building itself is put up. I've always made models of enterprises that I am involved with. It costs almost nothing, and just involves moving objects back and forth. It can save you a great deal of time, money, and frustration.

Just because you are not going to run a franchise operation does not mean that you can't look at a franchise restaurant for tips for your own eatery. If every table is laid out exactly alike, it suggests that these huge franchises have done time studies that satisfied them, and for which they doubtless paid a lot of money. Why fly in the face of such research? Use it. It can't be copyrighted—you can't copyright the height of a table or the space between two tables. If all these franchise operations use a timer for their French fries kettles, that ought to tell you something. Get a timer for *your* French fries kettle.

In manufacturing, the basics are important. Make certain that the floors are strong enough to support the machinery and workers. You need a guarantee of delivery of water, fuel, and power, as well as the sewerage capacity to get rid of your wastes. Make sure that it is available. The community, in its eagerness to have you as a taxpaying ratable, may overestimate its ability to deliver. You might want to pay an independent source to study whether the town can deliver on its promises.

Fitting Your Business Out

In buying equipment, as in other situations, knowing the field of endeavor helps. Asking around about where to get equipment is far more effective if you know people in the field. Garage sales, liquidation sales, Salvation Army sales—all are possibilities. Check classified advertising, especially in trade publications. (Such publications can give you many tips, including layout and design.)

You do not have to buy new equipment. You can buy used equipment for a quarter of the cost—shelving for a warehouse, racks for a gift shop, etc.—all available someplace if you know where to look.

This kind of search is best suited to metropolitan areas. If you're looking for used restaurant equipment, you will probably find fifteen dealers all gathered in a single square block of a major city. If, however, you live in West Overshoot, Wyoming, you have a problem. You will undoubtedly have to get to an urban center to find this sort of a district with the equipment you need. More than likely you'll have to rent a truck and haul the stuff back to West Overshoot. If you do happen to find the equipment in town, it will invariably cost more because of the lack of competition. You then have to decide whether it's worth your time and travel to look elsewhere.

If you are in the New York area and looking for display cabinets, for example, there's only one place to go—the Bowery. Little elves work there in fifty or more shops that nobody ever heard of. They do not advertise. You can buy display cabinets there at one-third the cost you would pay elsewhere. The bank check system, however, has never been introduced into that corner of the world. Everything is paid for in cash—no checks and no labels on the goods. There are districts like this one all over the country where you may buy the equipment you need, but you have to find them.

Your suppliers will help equip you if you know how to approach them. If you're opening a diner, for instance, don't buy a milk machine. The milk supplier will lend you a milk machine. He may not know it, but you ought to be able to talk him into it. The same applies to freezer cabinets and some display materials.

A Personal Note

One thing to remember from the start: don't go hunting for ducks in the Sahara. Match your customers with your product and your location.

While I was waiting for a few things to jell after college, I applied for a job driving for Mister Softee, a traveling ice-cream truck. The company had only one route available, and my interviewer was looking for a black man to take it because it wound through a black ghetto area that was considered difficult. I told him that if he couldn't find a black candidate, to get back to me, and about a week later he did. I took the route with enthusiasm, for it was just what I was looking for.

The second or third day that I was in business, I pulled up to a corner, and a big burly fellow began to climb into the cab. It was clear he didn't have my best interest in mind. I quickly picked up a roll of coins, clenched it inside my fist, and hit him in the jaw. He tumbled into the street. "Pass the word," I said to some people standing around. "Don't mess with Mister Softee." Things went well after that and I had no trouble.

My major problem was that Mister Softee made only chocolate and vanilla, and the clientele particularly requested strawberry. I bought vanilla mix, dumped strawberry syrup in the machine— instant success and sales zoomed.

Earlier, a friend and I had bought our own truck and converted it for ice-cream vending. We went into inner-city areas almost exclusively. Why? Because, we had found, that's where the real ice-cream money is. Even at half-past-ten at night there are still people on the stoops and in the playgrounds ready to buy. That kind of money could not be made ringing your little ice-cream bell in the suburbs. Those people are at the shore, or in the mountains, or in bed, but not on the streets.

DO YOUR HOMEWORK

Although I've been writing about getting started in business, many of the issues that have come up are involved in the entire life of a business from infancy to maturity, and so they will come up again later. One thought to end this section, however, seems vital.

I mentioned the New York photo store that "advertises heavily." Do you realize how much work is involved in those two words? It may have taken the business years to determine what mixture of ingredients maximized its success. When it was determined that the company should advertise and get an upstairs rental space, the owners still had to determine where to advertise. In which media? If in newspapers and radio stations, *which* newspapers and *which* radio stations? What kind of advertisements? Which products should be featured?

I've tried to express years of development in two words that cannot tell the whole story. This is important to you because you cannot assume that heavy advertising will make your business a success—you might sign a six-month contract with a newspaper only to find that your advertisements are not pulling, that you are wasting your money.

What I'm saying is that you have to do your homework. For any one of the topics I've touched on—floor layout, for example—whole books have been written on the subject, and you'll have to read those books. That may sound painful, but it isn't as painful as failure.

3

Skills and Trades

What's My Line?

From a very early age some people know, or at least think they know, what they are going to be doing with their lives. Other people spend much of their lifetimes thrashing about in trying to decide what to take up as a career or vocation.

I get calls on this dilemma from people on occasion, and the commonest response to my opening question is this: "I want to work with people." But that's just deliberately vague. If I mention getting into sales, the caller is liable to say he is not interested in sales. "Well," I'll suggest, "how about personnel?" No, that would mean that he would have to fire people and he couldn't handle that. "Working with people" does not mean much—it is often said just to have something to say.

Some people arrive at vocational decisions by the process of elimination—they discover, beginning rather early, what they *don't* want to do. My children helped take out our business trash and thereupon decided they didn't want to be garbage collectors. They worked behind the counter of our store and discovered they weren't interested in counter work. They loaded trucks and found out that they had little interest in being truck-loaders.

We all have some notions about what we don't want to do. I'm glad that people choose to become surgeons, because we need them, but there's no way that I'd want to be one. I find nothing attractive in such a profession.

Many people arrive at their vocational destination by default. They are offered jobs that they never considered or even knew about. Putting the pimentos into olives, for instance, is a job still done by hand. A young man needs work, looks in the newspaper want ads, and sees an opening at an olive factory. He winds up as a pimento specialist for the next forty years. He can't leave, or can't summon up whatever it takes to leave. He gets married, acquires a mortgage, some children, and a car. And he's stuck at the olive factory for the rest of his life.

As for myself, I never knew what I wanted to do when I was young. All I knew was that I wanted to be rich, I wanted to hustle, and I wanted to work for myself. At this point I think I'd like to be a 747 pilot, flying a big old wide-body around the world, but that's out of the question for me, for a whole bunch of reasons—not the least of which is my safety record.

Furthermore, I don't have the skills; flying big jets calls for the skills of a young person. It's true that the fellow flying the 747 is usually over fifty years old, because of seniority and union rules; he's been paying his dues for the last twenty-five years or more. This kind of flying is a career decision that has to be made early in life. If you want to be a commercial airline pilot you've almost got to make that decision in college. (A common route is to learn in the military service.) No matter how determined you are, if you're going to make a midlife career change at age forty-five, you're not going to become a commercial airline pilot, unless you buy the airline. What's more, I'm able to earn substantially more money doing other things.

Self-image is very much involved in occupational choices— you are expressing, with such choices, what kind of a person you believe yourself to be, or hope to be. Some people have strong choices and interests. Yet even here they may face a wide variety. A woman—or man—who is deeply absorbed in food and cooking, for example, may open a restaurant, or become a nutrition-ist, or write gourmet reviews for a newspaper.

Enjoying cooking and being a professional chef, however, are two different things. I met a fellow socially who was chef in a restaurant I had patronized and asked him for the recipe of a dish I had enjoyed. He began to oblige me by giving the ingredients: fifty pounds of flour, thirty-seven pounds of butter, and so on. When he realized from the expression on my face what he was saying, he remarked: "You know, I never thought about how to make it for two people."

Conversely, the young woman who makes that super coffee-chocolate dessert for six may not be able to make it for six hundred. That's a different league. There are all sorts of other considerations, such as how to do it at lower cost—will it work with dried eggs (at a fraction of the cost) rather than certified farm fresh eggs? Bakers, you know, buy egg yolks by the can. As a professional, concessions have to be made in terms of cost and efficiency, to which some people can accommodate while others cannot.

I'm suggesting that you have to take inventory of yourself when you're deciding what business to go into—what's realistic, what's impossible, what you like doing, and what you hate doing. You're making a decision that is going to take anywhere from forty to ninety hours per week of your time, so it really ought to be something you enjoy. It's foolish to launch into something that you're not suited to do. It's even more foolish to go out and do something you don't want to do. Finding out where you fit will take honesty and probably some luck.

The Varieties of Work

There are thousands of different kinds of jobs but only a few kinds of work.

Do you like tangible kinds of work? Work that you do with machines, tools, your hands, with plants, or with animals?

People who do this kind of work generally have good eye-hand coordination.

Do you like paperwork? Work that deals with data and needs clerical or arithmetic ability? This is detail-oriented work.

Do you like to analyze? Do you enjoy observing, experimenting, taking notes, solving problems? Most scientific work is of this sort. It's the work of researchers, consultants, report-writers.

Do you like creative work? People who like above all to innovate, use their intuition, and like to work in unstructured situations are led to this variety of work.

Do you like working with people? Most teaching and social work, providing information, training, and help involves working with people.

Finally, there's another kind of people-oriented work, but quite different—and that's what you might call enterprise work. It involves influencing people, performing, leading, and managing.

Thinking about where you fit in these categories ought to help settle some questions about your enterprise, and probably raises another set of questions.

Do you like to work in the physical company of other people, or do you prefer to work alone? Do you like to work in an office, a factory, a laboratory, or out-of-doors? Do you prefer working with tools or with your head?

Do you like to get a grip on intricate technical details, or do you prefer the give-and-take of meetings? Do you like to work set hours, or do you prefer to work when the mood suits you? Do you prefer that your work end with some concrete product, or do you like results that involve prestige or esteem?

Do you like working on long-range products (like the movies that used to be advertised "three years in the making"), or do you like to start a day with a new project and go home with it completed? Do you like to make presentations to convince others about the value of an idea or product?

Do you like to tackle things that no one else wants to touch? Does it bore you to see the same people every day? Do you like to tinker with different ways to allot work?

Do you like large enterprises or one-person operations? Do you like to supervise the work of others, or do you think of yourself as the Lone Ranger? Do you like to create your work by organizing and planning it, or do you prefer to have your next project walk in the door? Are glamour and attention important to you, or do you prefer anonymity and obscurity?

We tend to like to do what we do well. If you put arguments together well and express them clearly, you tend to enjoy debate; if you fall on your face in every argument, you tend to avoid debate. If you have a knack for fixing things, you fix things and thereby begin to learn more about machines; if you break everything you try to fix, you stay away from malfunctioning equipment and so learn nothing about it.

SELF-MANAGEMENT

Kinds of Skill

I've been talking about skill as if it were one thing, but there are really three basic kinds of skill. One kind is knowing your field, which people used to call know-how and now call expertise; the second is competence, your talent for accomplishing the job; and the third is self-management. By that I mean all the personal traits that make for success: punctuality, self-control, ability to pace yourself, good judgment calls, ability to work with people and delegate tasks, an understanding of and respect for deadlines—all those sorts of things.

Consider the problem of a certain highly-talented flower arranger. He could work hard, had fast hands, was very creative, and had the know-how at the source because he had grown up in the business. Unfortunately, he could not get along with customers. That was a major flaw. In a big operation, talented people who are deficient in some skills can still be used to advantage; the smaller the organization, the more difficult this expedient becomes.

We see this one-sided development of people in skills all the time; in fact most of us are "one-sided" to some extent. Artistic people, for example, are usually not profit-oriented. They may work to please themselves and spend so much time on a production that they can imperil their own business. A successful creative person probably needs a business manager, somebody who understands the bottom line—and like most bottom-line people probably understands nothing about creativity.

There's a lot of unnecessary concern about the perils of retraining people, especially the questionable maxim that after a certain age it's just impossible to retrain people. Some people can't be retrained at any age, while others are never too old to learn. Furthermore, some skills—the skills of self-management, for example—are easily transferred from one field to another.

It's as American as apple pie to change jobs; surveys show that more than half the people surveyed expected to change jobs within the coming five years. Nevertheless, people do tend to stay within a certain spectrum. A fellow may open seven different kinds of stores in a lifetime, but he's in the retailing business to stay. A young woman who starts in a computer-related industry is likely to stay with computers, although what she does in that field may vary widely.

Flexibility

I value it highly. Flexibility, which is a self-management skill, helps you to learn a new field and helps you to be prepared for whatever course your new enterprise may take—and your business will undoubtedly take turns you never expected. I have a friend who left a successful career in corporate life to go into the woodworking business, at which he is highly accomplished. His business has been successful, but quite different from the way he envisioned it. He had planned to make colonial reproductions, but whatever he has done in this area has been a sideline. His main source of work has been big orders from corporations for wooden items—wineries, for example, ordering several thousand wine gift boxes. So the business has taken on a life of its own.

Something of the sort may happen to your business. You think you're going to run an upscale operation and find yourself three years later running a bargain basement, because that's what worked for you. You start out as a retailer and begin selling to a group of other retailers and eventually find that you are running a wholesale business.

I can't stress strongly enough the importance of flexibility. If you're a retail-oriented person who likes to talk with shoppers and schmooze with wholesalers, you may be reluctant to get into supervisory work when the opportunity opens up. There's a lot more money in supervising ten stores than in standing behind the counter of one. (That's certainly true if you're an employee, and probably true if the business is yours.) As an employee, you're limiting your chances for advancement; as an entrepreneur, your chances for expansion. Perhaps you have some pretty convincing evidence that you lack the talent to be a supervisor. Okay, but then you will have to find another career path, or you're going to be a retail clerk for the rest of your life.

Employee skills. Incidentally, these skills which I've been discussing with regard to you are qualities to find in your employees as well. You'll have people who are ledger-sheet-oriented and others product-oriented. If the time clock breaks, you'll probably have an employee who can fix it. On the other hand, if the production of another employee is off by 50 percent, the clock-fixer probably won't have any notion of how to approach his fellow worker and set the problem right.

There are people who produce marvelously but whom you

will have to hide from the customers. And then you may come upon an employee who can walk up when Mrs. Smith—who is one of your major customers—is burning with indignation, talk it over with her, and have her leaving with a comment about what a great enterprise you have here. The natural schmoozer, with the smile and the arm on the shoulder, often has a great value in an enterprise. The people who are really good at it make a lot of money.

Self-discipline and Flexible Hours

If you have your own store and your hours are from 9:30 A.M. to 6 P.M., nobody is going to get you out of bed and tell you to be there at 9:30. The customer who goes to your store at 9:45 and finds that you haven't opened may never come back. It's a temptation, when it's ten minutes to closing time and nobody has walked through your door in an hour, to decide to close up and leave. It's a temptation, however, to be resisted. On the day you succumb to it, a customer invariably shows up who has driven five miles to get to your place, and is ripsnorting mad to find you closed.

And if you close at 6 P.M., what do you do about the customer who knocks at the door at five minutes past six? Do you let him in? I always did. When I was actively in the retail business— which was across the street from my house—I'd walk back over if I saw a car pull into the parking lot a half-hour after closing. I'd offer to open up the store just for them. This was not just to make a small sale. I did it because that customer might represent a big sale someday and might remember the service.

YOU AND YOUR ENTERPRISE

Wholesale vs. Retail

There's a world of difference between wholesale and retail and a great difference in temperament between the people in them.

The wholesaler works a lot closer on markup, but he sells five cases of peaches at a time. The retailer has to sell those peaches in 150 different sales and therefore has to have a higher markup.

Retailers are smooth. Wholesalers can be rough as a cob, and maybe they have to be.

For retailers, some of your clientele will be transient—people who will come into your store, make a purchase, and never be seen again. For the most part, however, your customers are local, and you have to cultivate a clientele within a relatively small circle. It's highly unlikely that anyone is going to drive for half an hour to buy a pair of shoes in your shoe store.

Wholesalers, on the other hand, may be in business all over the state, or even—if selling nonperishable goods—all over the country.

There's loyalty and good feeling at the retail level. If a woman likes the service at Jones Greengrocers, she does not mind paying a few cents more.

On the wholesale level, throats are slit for one-quarter of a cent per pound, and loyalties mean almost nothing.

Because their range is greater, wholesalers generally make more money. It costs more to get into wholesaling, however. Wholesalers may decide they just don't want to talk to a retailer and hang up on him—or her. Acting as though he doesn't need you is part of many a wholesaler's trade. Be prepared, when you visit wholesalers, to suffer indignities, obscenities and, if you are a woman, sexism.

Accepting the Environment

One night in a restaurant I met a certain businesswoman. She was in her mid-thirties, dressed in the high-necked blouse, floppy tie, and mannishly cut suit that proclaims that she is going to make it in a man's world. She was in an enterprise in which I have done considerable work. I was reminded of a story that was very appropriate to her situation.

59

In order to tell the story accurately, however, I would have had to use some language not suited to the drawing room. I wouldn't have used it to be offensive. Just as sometimes in a film nudity or expletives are necessary, this was a true story in which nasty language was necessary. And in deference to her, which was a mistake, I remarked that I hoped she wouldn't be offended by the language.

"I'm sure I will be," she said. (There were, incidentally, two other men at the table, representing an advertising agency, being very deferential to her.)

"Then I think that we have nothing in common," I said, "and that there's no way that we can do business. If you and I were going out for dinner tonight, I would expect to light your cigarette, open doors for you, and wait at the car door to help you in, because if I'm with a lady on a social basis I intend to treat her like a lady. But this is a business environment. You expect to be treated like an equal. Then you can't expect me to speak any differently than I would speak to the men sitting with you."

"Well, after all, I am a lady," she said.

"Then if you want to be different, don't expect to be equal in the business world," I said. "I'm prepared to treat a woman on an equal basis, because I think they deserve an even break in terms of business. But then don't ask for any quarter."

And that's where women are having a problem. They want to break in and sit themselves down in an all-male bar—and I fully appreciate that they don't want to be discriminated against—but then they have to accept where they are. The wholesale business, to take only one example, is a rough business, and it is not going to change to accommodate a woman. So if you can't take it, stay home with the kids. I have two daughters, and I would not want to see them discriminated against because of their gender. I make it clear when I'm doing business that I will never discriminate nor will I give quarter.

If you don't like rough language, you don't have to use it.

Some men are offended by strong language as well, and I say the same to them. It's an incidental thing that can so preoccupy you that you'll get mauled in business because you're worried about matters of relative unimportance.

Mail Order

People wandering about looking for some kind of enterprise to get into are often lured into the mail-order business. Magazines and newspapers are packed with advertisements claiming that a tiny initial investment is all you need to establish yourself in this lucrative field.

Well, those claims are all part of the mail-order business—the world of bronzed baby shoes, gimcracks, Social Security cards encased in plastic, clocks from Der Black Forest, and advertising novelties, as well as additives to gasoline that will enable you to drive around the world on eighty gallons. You will see a lot of these goods advertised by mail order; whether much of it is actually sold is another matter.

People buy by mail order because 1) it's a great bargain, or 2) it is locally unavailable, or 3) it's something that a customer would prefer not to walk in and buy (such as sexual apparatus).

In inaccessible rural areas, mail-order buying makes sense—if it's sixty miles to the nearest store, why not send for it? For that reason mail-order was a major method of retailing in nineteenth- and early twentieth-century America.

There are some good products sold by mail-order, but, a lot of mail-order is a game to fleece the chumps. A lot of the mail-order advertising that you see in the classified sections is being run *by* chumps who were enticed into investing in the machine that puts the plastic around the Social Security card; or they have sent in their $25 to learn how to make big bucks by stuffing envelopes, and what they have learned is that they have to run advertisements to try to entice *other* chumps to stuff envelopes. The ads are the same from month to month, but it's a different set of suckers running them. Most of these "make money stuffing envelopes" advertisements are the nearest thing to a pyramid scheme that you can get away with and stay on the right side of the law. The people who answer these advertisements are particularly susceptible. Many are housewives who can't leave the home because of young children, or people who have to stay home because of physical disabilities. Their desperation has made suckers of them.

Before you get into mail-order, examine with a grain of skepticism the people who want to help you make a lot of money. In most cases—the ones that are not actually fraudulent—these enterprises are unprofitable or at best only marginally profitable. You'd be better paid baby-sitting, and wouldn't work as hard. If the mail-order business is so lucrative, why do they need you? They need you, my friend, to sell you merchandise that you will sell elsewhere only with herculean effort. It's a way to sell you a $60 starter kit.

I am not saying that there's no money in the mail-order business. Most of it, though, involves large investments of capital.

One form of mail-order that seems to be thriving is late-night advertising on television. People are selling wok pots, oldies records, universal wrenches, and steak knife sets. Most of this stuff is overpriced. The people who are doing the advertising are not operating out of their garages. Production costs for the commercials are high; the broadcast costs are high as well, even at late-night rates and some are even advertised in prime time; and so is the 800 number to take calls from viewers. So this is not a field for the lightly financed. Not many people starting a business from nothing can afford this kind of overhead; if you start one, you'd better know what you're doing.

Multi-level Marketing
Another field that people looking for their own enterprises

tend to get sucked into is multi-level marketing. As in the mail-order field, the initial investment is quite manageable, and that's what draws people. In multi-level marketing, the person who recruits you gets a percentage of everything you sell. If you then recruit me, he gets a percentage, a smaller one, of what I sell. If I recruit Joe Brown, he gets an even smaller percentage of what *Brown* sells. The same principle works for you and me; the more people we recruit, the more money we make. Somebody who is in on this very early can make a lot of money on overrides.

Many people have described multi-level marketing as a pyramid system. The authorities look at it, therefore, with some suspicion. The courts have held that as long as an actual product is involved, it is not a full-fledged pyramid scheme. The similarities, however, should be obvious to the discerning observer.

People who recruit will frequently tell you that the real money in this field isn't in selling but recruiting. To be fair, the top people in the organization sometimes discourage this point of view.

Unquestionably there are people making money in multi-level marketing, selling cosmetics, vitamins and food supplements, and household cleaners. I suggest that if multi-level marketing works it has to sell products and not just recruit new people to buy starter kits. Here's a fair test of that. Let a multi-level marketer stop recruiting and just go out for three months and sell the product. Allocate a specific number of hours per day and see if you can make whatever hourly rate you think your time is worth—whether that's $50 an hour or $3 an hour—by selling the merchandise. If you can do that for three months, consistently, then you have demonstrated that the guys in the trenches can do it. Now you can legitimately solicit your friends, take them out, and show them that it's feasible.

Yet the way many people tell prospects that the real money is in recruiting doesn't stand up. They propose to their prospects that if the recruit gets 10 percent out of everybody he recruits, all he needs is ten recruits and he has cloned himself, making as much money as if he had worked himself. If everybody did that, they would soon have to be recruiting people in Shanghai and Peking, because we'd run out of Americans very quickly. If one person's ten people recruited ten, and each of them recruited ten, and each of them recruited ten, and each of them recruited ten, and each of them recruited ten, and each of them recruited ten, and so on for three more turns, that would make one billion people recruited, four times the population of the United States. So that's just a gimmick, in my view.

Some people make a lot of money in multi-level marketing, but I suspect that most people end up using the starter kit themselves—which is often good merchandise but rather over-priced.

How Many Dogs Can You Breed?

One problem about choosing your vocation is that you have to accept the consequences. A particular choice may mean that you have set limits to the amount of money you can make. That's fine—if you fully realize this. Take dog breeding as an example. Suppose you get $500 for a registered dog. You'll have to breed 200 puppies a year—which sounds like a lot to me—to gross $100,000. A lot of expenses, needless to say, come out of that gross income. And how many dogs can you realistically expect to breed and sell in a year? No matter how accomplished you are, it's likely that your income will be relatively modest—probably in the buying-a-job category. If, on the other hand, you open an ice-cream stand, there's nothing to prevent you from eventually owning 1,000 ice-cream stands.

That is the typical problem of the freelancer; that is, with the one-person operation. Of course many of them are successful. In a business card operation, for example, one person does everything: finds customers for the business cards, sets the type, orders the materials, runs them off on the offset printer, and makes the deliveries. It's a form of freedom that has its charms.

But if you go into a one-person business, what happens if you get sick? The whole thing evaporates. What if you are hurt in an accident and can't work for several months? Not only do you lack any means of support—unless you have disability coverage, which you had to pay for yourself, and is expensive—but your business dries up while you lie around in traction. You may have loyal customers who have been buying their rubber stamps from you for years, but if they need a rubber stamp, they will go somewhere else to get it. They can't wait until you are well enough to work again. Suppose the new place they go to is priced a little under your prices, or is a little closer. Or maybe the law of inertia goes to work—hell, they're buying from him now, why not stick with him? Lots of people freelance and have a prosperous time doing it, but the only way to do it is never to get sick.

I believe in businesses with employees (and I'm going to say more about employees later). If you have five people working for you, and you make 20 percent on each person's labor, those five people provide your salary, whether you are there or not. And that percentage is low; actually two or three employees ought to be providing your salary.

The Lure of the Islands

I said earlier that people tend to stay in the same field—in computers, or in retailing, or some other base around which a career revolves. That's generally so, but sometimes the exceptions are interesting. While I was in St. Croix not long ago, I met an attractive young woman as I got off the ferry who was trying to interest people in chartering her yacht for a day. While I waited for the next boat, I struck up a conversation with her, warning her that I was not a potential customer, but was curious. She was glad to tell me her story.

She and her husband were from New England, where he had been a dentist. They'd always liked sailing, so they decided to move down to the Caribbean and operate a charter boat business. The kids came with them. I expressed surprise that a flourishing dentist would give up his practice for such a chancy vocation.

Well, she said, he's on a dialysis machine, and we don't know how much time he has left, so we just decided to do what we really wanted to do. With all due respect, Boston certainly surpasses St. Croix in state-of-the-art medical facilities, so the decision to give up the dental practice and follow their star was obviously made with the heart as well as the head.

There is certainly nothing wrong with going into a new area, but I do urge that you do your homework and learn as much as possible about it.

If at First You Don't:

Some years back in a New Jersey mall, a fellow opened a shop selling quality chocolate. It was excellent stuff, hand-dipped strawberries and dainties like that. But the goods didn't move fast enough, and he had to go to a counter in someone else's shop. Then he opened a place on a major highway, in which basically he was wholesaling to shops. That didn't work very well either.

Eventually he tried specialty ice cream, much of it with his own candy sprinkled in it. And that turned out to be the right niche for him. Now he has stores in New Jersey, California, Washington, D.C., and Puerto Rico. People stand in line to get into his shops.

This fellow clearly had the right general idea but didn't quite get it right the first time, or the second time either. Sometimes that happens; it's one of the astonishing things about being an entrepreneur. You feel your way through it until you get it right.

So that's what finding your niche is about. Often it's acciden-
tal. Some people have a grand design, but for most of us, chance
and opportunity, and having those antennae waving in the air,
are what leads to getting in the right groove.

Franchises

There is a way that a beginner in business can acquire instant expertise and an instant, easily recognized brand name. It's called franchising, and although some people may not be familiar with how it works, it currently accounts for almost one-third of all retail sales in the United States. It's still growing, with the greatest growth in restaurants, rental equipment, printing and copying, and real estate.

No two franchise contracts are exactly the same, but generally a franchisee (the one who gets the franchise) has to pay a percentage of gross sales to the franchisor (the mother company) and help contribute to a national advertising campaign and to bookkeeping expenses. At the same time the franchisee owns his or her own business. This system has its advantages and its disadvantages; let's look at both.

ADVANTAGES

Predictability

A man is driving down the highway and feels a hunger coming on. On one side of the road he sees Smith's Hot Dog Stand; on the other, Howard Johnson's. He can probably recite the Howard Johnson menu from memory; he knows nothing about Smith's Hot Dogs.

Later that night he's getting tired and wants to find a place to sleep. On one side he sees the Beddiebye Motel; on the other, Holiday Inn. The Beddiebye Motel may be a great place, but he knows nothing about it. He knows exactly what to expect at the Holiday Inn; in fact for many years Holiday Inn advertised nationally that "the best surprise is no surprise." It's the same, from Maine to Los Angeles. Because of that predictability our traveler is likely to stop there. That brand identification helps mightily, especially if you have a transient trade.

Advertising

A franchise can tie your local operation to a national brand via local and national advertising. For example, Aamco, a large, national auto transmission repair and replacement franchise, uses cooperative local advertising (several franchises advertising together) to give a media mix of radio, television, and newspapers. Even if you had the money, you could never justify the expense of advertising your little business on a metropolitan TV station, because only one out of a thousand of the people who saw it could even find your place, much less want to patronize you. A cooperative TV advertisement, however, might be cost-justified.

Past Experience

The experience of the franchisor is also helpful. They know their product. The first franchisee to sign up with McDonald's showed amazing foresight. However, in those early days the organization did not have the vast resources that it now has as a matured operation to offer the beginner in hamburgology. Now, after years of experience, it has the number of French fries in a pound of potatoes down to an exact figure. They have laboratories that experiment with various kinds of oil to find the precise mix that makes the tastiest fries at the optimum price.

The experience of the company insures that you won't have to learn the hard way. These people know the angles that don't occur to beginners.

Suppose you are unaware that the highway on which you plan your business is slated to be widened and divided by a center island within a few years. The construction upheaval could cost you 90 percent of your business while the road is being completed and is for a time inaccessible. It also could cost you half your business permanently, since your place will be much harder to reach from the other side of the highway. No franchisor worth his salt would make plans for a retail operation on a highway without checking on the state's plans for the road.

Typically, the franchisor would also help in the building design, floor plans, equipment—items that baffle the inexperienced—and would offer continuing consultation on the operation of the business. Usually it will offer an extensive training program and helps its franchisees to set up an accounting system. It will help with the paperwork of applying for a loan and sometimes will even finance the project. Franchising is a good deal in many ways, and getting into it is betting with the odds, since the rate of failure of franchise businesses is lower than of small businesses as a whole.

Obtaining Supplies

Franchisors can also make your life easier in obtaining supplies by selling them directly to you. The law says, though, that they can only set standards of quality, and that if you can find the same quality elsewhere, you are free to use an alternate supplier. The franchisor must also tell you whether it is making a profit by selling supplies to you. Sometimes supply is the major value of a franchisor. This is the case in the muffler business, for example: the franchisor is able to buy more cheaply in bulk and can keep a wide variety of inventory on hand for you.

Lower Failure Rate

The reason for the lower failure rate is worth examining.

Many of the potential failures are winnowed out. The franchisor decided to drop an applicant because of his lack of experience, although training can of course partially overcome inexperience. The undercapitalized applicant is dropped because the company doesn't want to risk failure. A sound, established franchise may accept only two out of ten applicants.

Franchisees are sometimes rejected on the grounds of site selection. The franchise company pops the site data into a computer—so many high schools, so many teenagers, so many competitors within X number of miles, so much traffic—and if the answer comes up "TILT," don't bother to appeal. Computers are not infallible, but their results are coming surprisingly close. Conversely, the company will sometimes pick a site that seems to have drawbacks—such as an existing profitable operation on it that has to be bought out and torn down—and make a go of it when the computer says it will work.

The franchise companies have the formulas. Some types of people eat more fish than other types of people; therefore you can sell more fish at one location than at another—or designer jeans, or permanent waves, or hand tools. This kind of data helps the franchisors minimize failures.

(You can also do it yourself. This society has so much ready access to data that you can produce your own research on your own enterprise. You have to know, however, which data matters. Let's say you decide that your location has both the traffic and the surrounding population to support a new movie theater. You may have overlooked, however, that the average age of the residents of the area is sixty-five years, which may change the decision. Young people patronize movie theaters much more than do old people.)

DRAWBACKS

Although franchising has attractions, it may not be where you fit in.

Costs

First, when you join a franchise operation you have taken on a permanent partner. A percentage of every dollar you gross goes to the franchisor. That adds up to a hefty amount of overhead.

Furthermore, all these services and expertise are not offered to you free. They are built into the cost structure, and, as in any package deal, you may be paying for more than you need.

Restrictions

You will be restricted. People who left an employer to rid themselves of a boss may find that a franchise has wrested the management of their business from them—not completely, of course, but so many controls and requirements are set by the parent company that you may feel as rebellious as a teenager. The national sales office will dictate many of your special sales. You may think that you can get 110 cups from a pound of coffee, but if the parent company says 100 cups to the pound, there is no appeal board. You may not be able to offer certain items for sale if the franchisor disapproves. Your parent company may even establish a dress code for you—no blue jeans at work, for example. Do you want to take Sundays off? If the franchisor of your convenience store insists upon a seven-days-a-week operation, you will have to open on Sundays.

These directives can't be ignored; the effective franchisors employ checkers who stop by unannounced to make sure you are abiding by the rules. You can't bar them from the place.

As for the strictures that the franchises set up, unquestionably you can squeeze a few more cups out of a pound of coffee. You can even mix used grounds with the fresh grounds to stretch it a bit. But it will be more than your coffee that will suffer. The fellow who stops at your Big Doughnut franchise in East Orange, New Jersey, and decides that you must have given him a mixture of coffee and turpentine is not only going to write *your* place off—he'll probably be peeved with every Big Doughnut stop in America. The next time he's in Omaha, he's not going to stop at the sign of the Big Doughnut. That's why the franchisor wants all the coffee to taste the same, and from his point of view these are not empty rules but business imperatives.

Many years back I had a temporary job working for a lawyer, serving papers on franchisees of a dairy retail store chain. That was rather a hazardous occupation—handing a fellow a paper that told him Your Franchise Is Being Lifted. These were people who were diluting the soft ice-cream mix. They'd buy the mix in cans from the franchisor and stretch it a little with milk. The machine would freeze up just the same, and turn out a product in a cone that was perfectly pure and wholesome, but it was not the product that the company had devised: it had less butterfat. The company objected not just because it missed out on any royalty on the milk added to the mix, but because their product was being tampered with.

A company that does not enforce its standards may at first seem comfortable and easy to get along with. Its laxity, however, means that you as a franchisee are not getting all of what you are paying for—the uniformity and continuity of standards that is vital to the franchise concept. That represents a net loss to you.

The butterfat controversy occurred in reverse within Dairy Queen, a soft ice-cream franchise. The company decided to reduce the butterfat content in its mix to the point that it could not legally be called ice cream but was labeled ice milk. A number of franchisees who wanted to keep the product consistency spun off and reorganized as a new organization called Magic Fountain.

Extra Overhead

Above all else the most important question for a businessperson thinking about a franchise is the extra overhead it means. Will the franchise connection pay for itself? That's the basic question you have to answer.

Government Regulations

The government has become more stringent about franchises. Rules of the Federal Trade Commission require that a franchising company give its potential members a wide range of information about the company, its officers, and its history. The information comes either in a format designed by the FTC or in the FTC-approved Uniform Franchise Offering Circular, which is also used in several states that have their own franchising regulations.

This material should help you to undertake the extensive investigation you should make before committing yourself to a franchise. The material sent to you should include names and addresses of the nearest franchises in your area. Ask the owners some questions. Does the company deliver on its promises? Is the training worthwhile? If you had it to do over, would you sign on again?

Ask your banker and accountant if they have helped other clients get into a similar field. Go beyond the material the franchisor has provided: for instance, you might want to pay for a second, independent opinion on the company's site selection. A realtor or banker can provide you with the names of site selection consultants. Be suspicious if the company bridles at providing information. Be careful of a company that wants a lot of up-front money—how long has it been in the business, anyway? Beware of too much pressure, especially if the franchisor tries to dissuade you from seeing a lawyer. Don't be afraid to make business judgments; if the company continues to own some retail outlets while it converts others to franchises, is it just disposing of its own unprofitable units?

The disclosure statement will include a history of recent litigation and how the cases ended. Don't be put off too easily by the incidence of lawsuits; any company will have some suits by unhappy franchisees, and is likely to have to go to court to collect debts.

The franchisor must provide the disclosure statement before any money changes hands or any binding contract is signed, but does not have to give it to a prospective franchisee on first contact. A few franchisors, such as auto and oil companies, are not required to give such statements. If a company says it is exempt from this requirement, ask to see proof of the exemption.

Some agreements require that the owner-franchisee actively participate in the operation of the business, since the franchisors believe, and rightly, that it increases the chances of success. Some agreements give the franchisor certain prerogatives at repurchasing the franchise if you decide to give it up. *Right of First Refusal* means that if you have an offer from a purchaser, you have to tell the franchisor about it, and give the mother company a chance to match the offer dollar-for-dollar. If the franchisor does not wish to meet the offer, the business can then be sold.

Some franchisors place a straight buyback agreement in the franchise contract. That means that if you want to sell you must sell it back to the franchisor at some agreed-upon formula in the contract, probably based on the gross income. I would stay away from such franchisors.

The Right of First Refusal does not harm you financially. As for a buyback, however, you can bet that any formulation worked out by the franchisor is to its advantage and to your disadvantage.

As a result of the federal government's close watch over franchises, the latest development has been to obtain the same result by means of some other legal route, such as a limited partnership. The company sidesteps the franchise law by cutting itself in as your partner.

CONCLUSION

Franchises are not for everybody or for every situation. The case for a franchise becomes weaker if you are depending largely on local regulars as customers. The major benefit of many franchises is their attraction for transients—people who have never heard of you but know your product.

On the other side, you are never truly independent as a franchisee. You always have to phone mother. If a disagreement arises, mother is usually going to win, one way or another. Not only because the mother organization has more clout and more money, but because it would rather rid itself of you than lose to you. If it loses to you, it has lost to all its franchisees.

One last point to remember: a good franchisor sincerely wants you to succeed. It makes money on your success and a failure hurts the whole organization. Some franchisors, however, are not really interested in the long pull, but in getting their up-front money and saying good-bye. The get-in-and-get-out franchisors rely heavily on fads, so you have to ask yourself whether this is a fad that will soon become last year's novelty, or is it a long-range business with a future? Ask that question of the people holding the franchises, too. If the company is set for the long haul, it wants you to succeed, will get behind you to help, and that increases your chances of success.

TWO FRANCHISE EXPERIENCES

Franchising for Billboard Space

The Red Bull Inn, a New Jersey motel, had already been successful for nineteen years when its partners married it to the Best Western franchise in 1983. Although his partner had been interested for years in joining a franchise, Jory Levine had remained opposed, until the available space for the motel's billboards began to contract. The billboard company, favoring a strategy of national rather than local advertising, eliminated more than half of the motel's outdoor spots and intended to eliminate more.

"We were bluntly told that within a few years we'd have

nothing," Levine said. "The advertising people would overprice them so that we couldn't retain the contracts." The inn, he said, was getting 15 percent of its measured reservations from billboard advertising.

The partners agreed on Best Western because the affiliation is looser and all the units do not have to look alike. The money that would have gone into billboards was reallocated into the franchise. "So financially it didn't disturb us at all," Levine said. "It was only my own ego that was bothered in the slightest."

Six months after signing up, Levine found mostly plusses on his scorecard, although he expressed a dislike for the Best Western billboards and said that the computerized reservations system did not bring any additional business to the inn. Almost all the reservations coming through the new system were old customers using the system to make a free telephone call, he said.

His overall positive view of Best Western was based on its inspections, which he called bracing, and on the support that the franchisor contributes with various kinds of expertise. One of the company's specialists, he said, proved invaluable in helping him replace his switchboard with the latest in direct dial telephone service to guest rooms.

A Study in Pressure

Some years back I decided to break into the movie theater business. If you're familiar with it you know that the major sticking point in the business is getting the films. You are not going to get first-run films unless you have some leverage, and without first-run films you are not going to attract audiences.

At that time Jerry Lewis Cinemas was advertising in *The Wall Street Journal* and elsewhere as a new franchising venture for movie-house owners. I called the company, and the first question I asked was about access to first-run films. I was told that the company was putting together a large nationwide chain that would have the leverage to get the films. This made abundant sense to me.

I liked what I was hearing, and when I went to meet with representatives of the franchise company I was impressed. I sat with them at a table on which you could have played hockey, except that it would have spoiled the highly polished finish. The salesman moved in immediately to establish a first-name basis; let's call him John. He was a well-turned-out fellow, bald and bearded, distinguished and suntanned.

John told me that the deal for franchisees was $10,000 up front; in the 1960s, when this occurred, $10,000 went a lot farther than it does now.

When I arrived home and studied the promotion package, I was favorably disposed.

Several more conversations followed. I concluded a lease arrangement with the people who owned the property on which I was planning to build. On Friday I had a $10,000 certified check ready to send to Jerry Lewis Cinemas.

That same afternoon John called. "I have to tell you," he said, "that the fee is going up to $15,000 on Monday."

"Is that right?" I replied.

"Yes," John said. "Look, the only reason I'm calling you is because I like you. We got along well. If you get your check in the mail, postmarked before Monday, you're in for $10,000. But if it's Monday, it's going to cost you $15,000."

"Gee, thanks for calling," I said.

After hanging up, I walked over to my secretary's desk. "Do you have that check we got this morning at the bank?" I asked. She handed it to me and I tore it in half.

"Take this back to the bank," I said, "and get us credited for $10,000."

I had become immediately suspicious when a man I hardly knew called me up to do me a $5,000 favor because he liked me so much. Why would he have such an intense liking for a person he hardly knew? I felt I was being hustled. Undeniably people do business favors for one another out of fellowship, but not on such short acquaintance. If John and I had been associated for a long time, there would have been little question about the call.

John's phone call saved me a bundle of money, because the company went broke shortly thereafter.

In any kind of business deal, franchise or otherwise, be suspicious when the pressure is applied. Don't be hustled.

Incidentally, right smack in the neighborhood of where I planned mine, a very successful movie theater is playing first-run movies.

5

Start-Up Money

Sometimes when you don't have money you have to rely on nerve. That's how we got into the nursery school business back in 1961. One day in Philadelphia I walked into a supply house for nursery schools and began to select things off the floor. "I'll take ten of those," I said, "and two of those . . . and three of those."

The owner was beaming as if I had made his month. He would not have been nearly as happy had he known that everything I had in the world was outside in our station wagon, and that included three kids. When the buying splurge was over he asked me how I would be paying. "Well," I responded, "I expect thirty days."

Not quite as blissful as before, he said that he would have to have something down. I offered ten percent. I had already been figuring the arithmetic mentally as my bill mounted, and I knew I could just make ten percent, although it would break the piggy bank. I drove out of Philadelphia with all my nursery school supplies, purchased at ten percent down, courtesy of a man who'd never seen me before in his life.

He waited three years to be paid.

At first he would call up and yell: "I WANT MY MONEY!" That failed to work. My then-wife functioned as a buffer, taking most of the abuse. (It's a comfort to spread the abuse.) She played the nice half of the family partnership, which is in character for her. After a while the Philadelphia creditor developed an affectionate telephone relationship with her. "Ruth Ann," he would ask, "do you think you can get him to send me some money this month?"

"I'll do my best," she'd say. Later she'd tell me we would have to send him some money. He was paid every nickel he had coming, but it took him a while to get it.

A couple of months after the nursery school opened, we were totally strapped. I was too proud to go to my parents or my in-laws, and as a practical matter neither set of parents had much money. It happened that a new loan company office was opening in a nearby shopping center. Five minutes after the ribbon was cut, I was passing by. I surmised that no established finance company in North America would even give me the time of day at that point in my fortunes.

I figured, however, that this guy might be hungry. He looked it. He was standing out in the morning sunshine in front of his office. I slowed down as I neared him and remarked that I was waiting for the bank to open. "It's already open," the manager said.

I said excuse me, my watch must be wrong.

"How are you doing?" he asked. "Do you need money?"

I asked him what I would need money for.

"Well," he responded, "we could all use money, couldn't we? Let's go inside and talk about it."

The talk within soon came to focus on a $500 loan, which was the maximum that a small loan company could lend in those days. The interest, the height of exorbitance in the early 1960s, was 18 percent, but I didn't care about the rate at that moment. I was only interested in the monthly charge. "Do you have any collateral?" he asked me.

Well, I said, that would probably be the furniture.

"May I see it?" he asked.

I took him to our living quarters, in the rear of the nursery school, and asked my wife to show him through all sixteen rooms of the house. It was crammed with high-quality furniture and lavish Oriental rugs. The whole caboodle was probably worth $100,000. I never told him that I owned *this* furniture. It belonged, as a matter of fact, to the landlord, who was about to move out and take it. All Ruth Ann and I owned was a wheezy refrigerator. My creditor apparently jumped to the unwarranted conclusion that this was our furniture, and lent me $500. That loan kept us afloat for a few more months while the nursery school got started.

BORROWING MONEY

Money is the fuel that makes an enterprise run, and beginning businesses need start-up money that invariably involves going into debt. Borrowing money to purchase equipment to be used over the long term is perfectly sound practice, and is common in both government and business. In your case you are borrowing money called *venture capital*—that is, money lent for a new and untried enterprise.

Banks

For most people, the first place that comes to mind when borrowing is mentioned is a bank. If you already have a sound, proven business, there's nothing to prevent you from borrowing money against *that* business to start another one. If Business B goes under, Business A will ante up, or be liquidated, to cover the bank's position. The bank, however, is not going to lend you venture capital in any great amount unsecured; if you want to mortgage the family homestead, you can probably get a loan that way. It's not a sure thing, however. In states that have a Homestead Law (Texas is one) it's impossible to mortgage your home

83

to start a business, because the law forbids the bank to lend for that purpose.

Let's say you decide to mortgage the house to borrow money from a bank to establish a beauty parlor. Suppose you tell the bank officer: "I'm going to leave my job to set up this new beauty parlor, and I need $25,000 to get started." You have probably guaranteed a rejection.

You should not lie to the banker. If you want the money for a beauty parlor, but tell him you want it for an addition to your home, that's a lie. Not volunteering everything, however, is not the same as lying. It's an omission. If he did not ask you whether you intended to stay at your job, it hardly seems necessary for you to blurt out information that squelches your chance for a loan.

As for borrowing from a bank, you can probably skip it anyway. Banks are not ordinarily in the business of lending venture capital, and for good reason. Banks are not lending you their own money, with which they would be free to gamble, but the hard-earned savings of their depositors, over which they are merely custodians. Federal agencies guarantee and insure these deposits. The FDIC restricts the banks considerably. The banks have a little flexibility, but they are allowed only so many bad debts, and if they go over the limit they've got a serious problem. They are not in the business of speculating with depositors' money. The function of a bank is to provide capital for proven enterprises for expansion, not to provide venture capital for new entrepreneurs.

But don't pass up an opportunity for a bank loan. Some banks periodically solicit people for a homeowner's line of credit. You can borrow against the equity in your home, on a secondary mortgage basis, at a fairly competitive interest rate. Sometimes there's a one-time application fee, but the banks often waive the fee. It's smart to apply for that loan when you *don't* need it. It does not matter whether you borrow or not, the point is that the money is there and you don't have to go in for it wearing knee pads.

Where Else to Look

Banks probably will not lend you money, and finance companies don't lend in the amounts you're looking for, so where should you get the loan? Except for loan sharks, anywhere you can.

Family. Twenty-five years ago I would never have said that. I would have said, don't borrow money from your family. That's all changed now. I never borrowed any money from my parents, but I would never hesitate to lend money to my children. That does not mean that I'm more stalwart and self-reliant than they are; it just means that times have changed.

When I was trying to borrow, money was being lent at 5 percent interest. I took out a third mortgage at one time at a rate then considered usurious—actually it was illegal—of 7.5 percent. That was in 1963. Now an interest rate of 7.5 percent is read about in the history books. So if your parents are going to lend money to the bank at 8 percent, and you're going to borrow it back from the bank at 14 percent, why not just borrow it directly from your parents and eliminate the middleman? You can give them 9 percent interest, and everybody benefits.

Your agreement with your parents, however, or with any other family member or friend, shouldn't just be based on a kiss or a handshake. A note should be drawn up specifying the terms of the loan. The loan should be recorded in a businesslike fashion. Life is too uncertain to handle it otherwise.

Suppose, for instance, a daughter comes to her parents for a $10,000 loan for real estate, and the parents just give it to her without any record of any sort. The loan is not yet repaid at the time the daughter and her husband decide to round out their marriage with a divorce. The son-in-law has an interest in that real estate. Now if the loan had been somehow recorded—as a mortgage or even as an I.O.U.—the parents would have clear rights to recovery of their money. But if there is no record, the daughter may say she intends to give the $10,000 back to her parents, and her husband can say, "That wasn't a loan, but a gift, and half of it belongs to me." Or what if the daughter dies? Now the son-in-law has the money, and may say that he doesn't know where his wife got the money.

Life insurance. So you don't have parents to borrow from. Do you have a life insurance policy? You may have built up considerable equity that you have forgotten about, and since it's your own money, the interest rate is highly favorable. If you're leaving your job, you may be cashing in a pension plan, or you may be able to borrow against it. Check the tax implications before you act.

The seller. Another source you may tap—and this has become standard practice—is the seller, if you're buying an existing business. Most sellers today expect to carry paper. (Now what does that expression mean? It means that when the prospective buyer is unable or unwilling to put all the money up in cash, the seller agrees to take at least a portion of the payment over a period of time.)

A quarter of a century ago few sellers were carrying paper. The seller would expect you to come to him with the financing all prearranged, and if you walked in and suggested that he take part in the financing, the door would have been slammed in your face. Time and high interest rates have changed all that.

If the seller will *not* carry your paper, if he wants payment in full, you ought to get a bargain. That happened to my son Matthew and me when we were looking for a service station and auto rental property. A fellow called me up and said he heard we were looking. Why didn't you call me? he asked. I said, because I heard you're looking for cash and I want somebody to carry me for ten years.

He said he could not do that. He and his brothers were dividing an estate. It was his task to settle the estate, and he and his brothers were not overcome with fraternal affection for one another. He didn't want to administer the payments for ten years; he wanted to get out of it quickly. That was all right with me, but under those circumstances I did not expect to pay anything like I would on a deal in which he would help carry me. So we got the land at a fire-sale price, for about half of what similar properties were going for—by mortgaging another piece of property to come up with the cash.

With the seller carrying your paper you will be paying more, but that's because you're using someone else's money. That's all right if it works. As long as the enterprise will throw off enough to retire the debt plus provide a reasonable profit for your labors, what difference does that make? Pay 50 percent for money, if necessary, if you can then get 55 percent for it somewhere else, but don't pay 5 percent for it if you can only get 4 percent for it. The *spread* is what matters, the difference between the percentages.

Don't get hung up on the terms, either. Terms, however good they sound, are no good if you can't make the payments. Even if the seller offers to carry you at no interest, the business still has to generate enough money to pay him. Suppose the seller offers you a business at no interest, just a payment of $2,000-per-month installments, but the business only throws off $1,200. Where does the other $800 come from?

Advertising for Money

If you can't come up with the start-up money yourself, and the seller won't carry your paper, or if you are planning a completely new enterprise, one way of finding money is to advertise for it. Take a classified advertisement in the "Capital Wanted" column of a major newspaper (*The New York Times, Wall Street Journal* or the like). A lot of people out there want to invest money, and it's worth looking into.

Don't give your prospective lenders a lot of unsolicited information, but send them enough to elicit a response. Tell them your intentions succinctly. For instance: "I'm going into the chocolate-chip cookie business. I have ten years' experience in the field. I have an option for a mall location in the Orangeburg Shopping Center, in a trade area of 500,000 people." The fact that you have taken out an option for a site, that you've done something positive, ought to interest a venture capitalist more than a solemn recounting of your intentions.

When I went into the nursery school business in 1961, I ran a classified ad in the *Wall Street Journal*. I found a colonel in the Air Force who had inherited money and was looking to invest it, but that failed to work out. I eventually borrowed money through an attorney representing a couple who had inherited a lot of money from a European relative they knew nothing about. They were working people who had never handled large amounts of money, so they had worked out an agreement with the attorney to buy out mortgages at high (in fact usurious at the time) rates of interest.

Some of the money that's out there as venture capital is funny money—hidden in mattresses, on which people have never paid taxes. Some of it isn't even funny. In response to my *Wall Street Journal* ad, I had a fellow walk into my living room with a briefcase full of bright green cash. "How much do you want?" he asked me. I couldn't wait to get him out of the house. Obviously I was being offered underworld money.

That kind of money is still around today, but I would not advise getting involved with it. For one thing, the mob lacks sympathy about your inability to repay. They don't intend to let you pay the debt off; they want to own you. Little enterprises like yours can be used to launder money and do other favors. I have never borrowed money from such sources, and they are hardly my choice of business associates.

Some companies have gone into the business of investing venture capital to finance new ideas—as well as patent them, produce prototypes, and market them—but they do not much deal with individuals. They are companies dealing with companies. Any venture capital you will find doubtless comes from individuals—dentists, physicians, lawyers, highly paid corporate people—who earn substantial sums of money in their own fields and want to put some of it to work at a higher rate of return than they would expect to get in a conventional money fund or even in a stock investment. They are not interested in a 10 or 15 percent return on their investments; they expect to be rewarded well. They are entitled to big rewards because they are taking bigger risks, and many of the investments they make go down the tube.

If you hope to attract venture capital, you must be prepared to give something up. You will have to pay a lot of interest, or give up a piece of the business, or some combination of both. I prefer to pay the interest. If I really think I have an enterprise that will eventually be highly successful, I'd rather give up the interest; then the business will ultimately be mine alone. That means a substantial sacrifice in interest, but it's worth it to me.

If I were a lender, on the other hand, I wouldn't take interest alone. Unless I got a piece of the business I would not be interested. Some venture capital people are interested in nothing more than a decent return on their money, but increasingly they want a piece of the action. That's where the real money will be. They want to be in either as a minority partner or a minority stockholder.

The major problem for you in that kind of arrangement is not what you give up in money, but that you have lost your absolute control of the enterprise—you're not an owner any more, but a partner. When you have a partner you have accountability—

beyond, that is, your accountability to the IRS. If you own your enterprise completely, and you decide to attend a seminar in Hawaii, and the seminar meets the IRS guidelines, you just sign up and go. With a 20 percent junior partner, however, you may still have the power to make such a decision, but you may have somebody jumping up and down and making angry sounds. "What do you mean, you spent $5,000 on a two-week seminar?" he may shout over the telephone. "One thousand of that was mine!"

If you and the venture capital prospect agree on the enterprise but disagree on the details, try to negotiate. You might try to work out a buy-back agreement so that you could eventually shed your partner at a price that would be attractive to him— possibly at 150 percent of the book value of his share. You might buy it back in a way that would create a tax benefit for him. The key, as in all agreements, is that the deal must benefit both parties, sometimes called a yes-yes deal.

You might also find a way to put him on the payroll and give him perquisites, all of it within the legal bounds of IRS rules. Any legitimate benefit that finesses the taxman could be entertained.

Tax advantages are another bargaining chip. A new venture in all likelihood is going to lose money in its initial years. Out of these losses can come some serious tax advantages for which you have no use. The Peoria dentist who lent you the money may be in a higher tax bracket and may have use for such losses. It's unlikely that you can apply these losses against a later profit, so it costs you nothing to give them up anyway; and even if there is some advantage for you somewhere down the line, it's a small price to pay. This is a sweetener that can make the difference and can be passed along by means of a partnership agreement.

Last Resorts

If all else fails, you can try the government. The Small Business Administration in the federal Department of Commerce makes loans. You have a better shot at it if you are a member of a minority group—black, Hispanic, or female—but even here the little businesses don't fare well. The SBA for the most part is not interested in making $10,000 loans for tiny projects; it has somewhat bigger deals in mind.

There's also the last resort of coming up with money by using your credit cards. Some people have handfuls of these cards, and can borrow on each one. The rates are exorbitant—as high as 22 percent—but if that's the only way, it's possible if the amount you need is modest, and it beats dealing with the mob.

And then there's the possibility of getting someone to co-sign a loan.

Co-signers. I want to digress for a moment because this question comes up so often when people call my radio show. A co-signer is the same as a signer, as far as the lender is concerned. If you co-signed for a bank loan, the bank does not care that "I co-signed but Harry got the money." As far as the bank is concerned, *you* got the money. If it's easier to collect the money from the co-signer, that's who the bank will go after. Bear in mind that you are completely responsible for the loan, not proportionately responsible.

Nevertheless, if this is the only way a bank can be induced to lend you money, you ought to consider it. You might ask your parents to co-sign a loan rather than borrow directly from them. In fairness to your parents, you ought to explain exactly the jeopardy in which they put themselves by doing so. If they elect to do it, then they have knowledge in full of what they are doing.

Good luck in your search for start-up money. I hope I didn't make it sound easy, because it's not. Financing for the million-dollar projects is easier to find these days; for the average entrepreneur with more modest needs, this is a difficult historical period.

OTHER WAYS OF OBTAINING MONEY

The Other Side of the Equation

The problem with borrowing money on your home to finance a venture is this: now you have not only the original mortgage to pay off, which can be a struggle in itself, but you have a second mortgage payment to make. There is an alternative. You can sell your house. Then you have no mortgage payment to make it all. You will have working capital for your business. You may rent quarters, or you might move back in with your relatives. Sometimes it is possible to move right into the building that houses your business. "What!" I hear so often when I mention this, "and drag my lifestyle down ten notches?" The only response I can make to that is: how badly do you want to go into business for yourself?

There's another alternative. Suppose you have $100,000 in equity in your home. Suppose it's possible to borrow $80,000 on that equity, although you really only need $40,000 for start-up money. You can borrow the entire $80,000, use the $40,000 for the business, and use the other $40,000—which you will of course have invested—to pay off the second mortgage payments over the first couple of years, when the going will really be tough. This will take some of the money pressure off your shoulders at a time when you'll be facing other business pressures. Now, that's not a method of first choice, or maybe even third choice, but it gives you an alternative to giving up the search for capital. The question is how badly you want to become the owner of a business.

We lived upstairs for years in the back rooms of the nursery school. It was almost free. We didn't have to pay any rent. We had to heat the building whether we stayed in it or not. The extra utilities we used came to only a small cost. It represented an enormous saving at a time that we needed to conserve our capital. We left a very comfortable Cape Cod four-bedroom home for an upstairs backroom environment, cooking in the same kitchen in which we prepared the school lunches.

Such a tremendous change would be more wrenching for the lady of the house than for most husbands, who are generally slobbier by nature and for whom housepride is less important. Many women just could not stand it—and that's not a criticism of them but an observation. It was a tremendous comedown for us, but it was necessary so that we could accomplish what we wanted to do. Furthermore, we knew that it was a temporary situation that would end someday.

A Penny Saved

I don't think that anyone can separate the subject of raising capital for a new enterprise from the related subject of scrimping and saving during those early years of getting the enterprise afloat. Everything that you save is in effect raised capital, money that can be funneled into the business.

We used the minibus as our family car. None of us were enthusiastic about that, but it got us from one place to another, and it cut down on car payments. You may protest, "I can't pull up to a friend's house in a pick-up truck." Well, I can tell you that it helped us to survive. I can also tell you that my successor, the fellow who bought the nursery school from me, did the same thing. For several years he and his family used the minibus as *their* family car. Now he drives around in a good-looking automobile. When he was saddled with the huge payments that starting a new venture entails, he made the same sacrifices that we had made before him.

Raise capital for yourself. If you're working one job, get a second job. Perhaps your spouse can get a job as well. All that money goes into the kitty. You'll be surprised how much money you can squirrel away in a couple of years, if you are single-minded.

Let's say you've left a successful career as an executive to become a consultant, and the early going is rough. Nobody has to know that at 10 P.M., when no one is about, you and your spouse come into the office, vacuum the carpets, scrub the floors, and clean the toilets. If janitorial service costs you $100 a week, you have increased your cash flow by $100 by doing it yourself.

I know that's not the kind of advice that people want to hear. "I've got a master's degree in business," someone will puff, "and you think I'm going to scrub toilets?" Or: "My wife's too tired to do that." I'll bet, however, that if you were really able to get at the truth, you'd discover that most successful entrepreneurs cleaned toilets at one time or another.

You will notice that I didn't suggest that you save money by functioning as your own lawyer. Cleaning up the office is not going to cost you anything but time and doesn't require a skill that you lack (with all deference to professional janitors). I also would not say that you should drop your accountant and do it yourself. You might do your own posting, or perhaps your wife stays home to do the posting while you clean the office. Keep your accountant.

The drudge work, however, you can do. Don't advertise that you do it—not that it's anything to be ashamed of—but it is not necessary for anyone to know. It's an ephemeral situation, a means to an end. If you're going to be doing your own floors for the next forty years you're in the wrong business—you're doing something wrong. For five years, however, it might be necessary.

Turning Liabilities into Assets

You can use your limitations as a style of your own. Say you open a steak house. You can go out and buy expensive table settings, and maybe that's the ambience you want to create. On the other hand, have you ever been to a restaurant where the drinks come in jelly glasses? And the forks are all different patterns? One plate is blue and another green?

That restaurateur can equip his or her place for five percent of the cost of new stuff. You can buy it at flea markets and penny sales. And people will comment about how interesting all this oddball stuff is. Obviously, there are environments in which this will fall on its face. There are others in which it will work. People will pass the word about the great offbeat restaurant with the jelly glasses. You might find glasses with all kinds of emblems on them. You can buy chairs for a few dollars at a garage sale instead of paying $75 or $100 each for them. Old boards and old signs are very fashionable nowadays. And if you have a big wall to cover, you can go to an auction and buy books for a penny or so a volume. Saving money takes creativity.

When I first opened the nursery school I was taking a course at Rutgers University. It was one of those courses with thousands of students in it—and it turned out that the professor sent his children to our school. One day he told the class about it. "My kids go to the most unique nursery school around," he said. "The fellow who owns it drives up in a station wagon and the kid who's getting out next is always sitting in the front seat. He reaches over and picks him up under his arms and puts him out the front window of the driver's side into his mother's arms. All the kids get a big kick out of it."

Yes indeed, that was a trademark of mine. And why do you suppose I did it? Because I couldn't open the front door of the car. It was a new station wagon, but my son Mark, who was then about a year and a half old, had put the car in reverse in the driveway one day and wiped out the left front door. It snapped the hinges. The door lay on the ground. I discovered that you can put the door back in place, that the hinges have nothing to do with keeping a car door in place. They only come into play when you open the door. For a year I could not afford to get the door fixed, so I drove up and handed the children out the window. Even after the door was fixed, I was stuck with this little stylistic gesture. It was a liability that had been turned into an asset.

Defer Payments

Putting off payments until the future is not really a saving. In fact it costs you money. Sometimes, however, it can help you get through an early tight-money period. Suppose that you need a piece of equipment for your business that costs $7,000. You are able to make a deal with the supplier to defer payments for a year, but you will have to pay $8,500 then. That's $1,500 in interest—a lot to pay on $7,000. It may be more to your advantage, however, to pay the interest than to tap yourself out before the business has a chance to get started.

Minimize Your Obligation

To help you make it in your new enterprise, it's wise to pare down your obligations as much as possible. If you are paying the minimum on your credit cards every month, pay them off and pack the cards away where they won't be a temptation to you and you won't have payments to make every month. If you have a relatively new automobile, sell it and pay off the loan. Even though you may take a loss on the sale and pay extra on making the car payments early, it's $250 or so per month that you won't see flowing out. The savings in insurance will also be considerable.

Sometimes you can live on less when you stop going to work. You may use the car less, work in old clothing, eat lunch at home. In other kinds of business, however, your expenses may increase because of your need to maintain an image; if you drive up in an old car in some businesses, you have signaled that you are not doing well. That's no reason, however, that your spouse has to drive a fancy car.

(In some businesses it doesn't pay to have a good car. A very successful butcher in my neck of the woods used to buy a new Cadillac every two years, but he kept a disreputable piece of junk that he drove to work and parked in front of the butcher shop. He did not intend to let his customers know that he was making such good money; they'd think he was charging too much.)

I would never suggest that you drop your life insurance coverage—but you might consider converting a whole life policy into a term policy, which would cost a lot less and still give your family protection. While it's pleasant to belong to the country club, you can give it up—unless it's a proven asset for business contacts.

One of the things I gave up, which was painful to me, was Friday night poker games. They were not low-stakes games, and you could get hurt; on a given night you could lose a week's pay. I came to the conclusion—and this was well into my business career, when I was doing some expanding—that I could not afford to lose a week's pay. I played well enough to win it back the next week, but the money was too tight for that kind of a loss, even temporarily. I hated giving it up for two reasons: first, because I loved it, and second, it was even more difficult to tell the guys I was playing with that I couldn't afford it. But it was equally difficult for my wife, who had excellent taste and standards in clothing, to start buying synthetic fabrics.

Every dollar by which you decrease your expenses is equal to a dollar by which you have increased your income.

A good exercise to try: get a notebook and for a month write down every single penny you spend, and by means of this locate your leaks. You'll be surprised at how the money drains out. Write down items that you can drop—you can read one newspaper instead of three, do without a telephone extension, call your parents once a week instead of twice, eat out less often, go to the movies less frequently. You and your spouse may enjoy the movies more when you have to choose them carefully. Someday, if you're successful, it won't matter how often you go, how often you eat out, or how many newspapers you purchase. These savings now will help that day to arrive.

The fact is that for small enterprises, in their early stages, 99 percent of the help has to come from within—from the end of your arm, your family, or close associates. The ability to borrow without collateral is becoming minimal. That's just the way it is these days. Despite these obstacles, people are still starting their own businesses and making successes of them.

6

Which Way to Go?

One of the first questions that comes up with a beginning entrepreneur is whether it would be suitable to incorporate. In my opinion every successful business should incorporate at some point—and many should do so even before they are successful.

The prime reason for incorporation, even for a fledgling company, is to place a corporate shield between yourself and the liabilities that the business may develop. I'm not talking primarily about business expenses, such as the purchase of equipment and supplies. I'm talking about involuntary liabilities that might arise, such as lawsuits in which your product may be blamed for having made someone's hair fall out. We'll talk about this again later, but I must stress that it is indispensable to the protection of your house and other possessions.

If you are really pressed for money, it may be possible to avoid incorporating for a time—since it costs money, requires the services of a lawyer, and takes some paperwork. Nevertheless, you are running an additional calculated risk by not taking immediate advantage of the corporate shield, so I'd consider doing it very early in your career if not at the outset. Furthermore, incorporating also creates advantages in perquisites and fringe benefits that will be discussed later.

Naming Your Enterprise

Every fictitious name has to be registered. You do not have to incorporate to create a name for your business, but you do have to register it. In most states unincorporated trade names are registered in the office of the county clerk (this office is known by other names in some states, but the function is the same). Registration of your name gives you the exclusive right to use that name in that county. If you use your own name as the business name you do not have to register the name, nor do you have to register a partnership that uses the full name of the partners, such as Stanley Abbott and Sylvester Costello. If you use the name Abbott and Costello, however, it must be registered, because those are not full names. And if you call your business Stanley Abbott Widgets, that has to be registered.

The county clerk would raise no objection if a Howard Johnson were to open a restaurant and call it Howard Johnson's. The national company with that name might object, however—so you might run into a lawsuit about it even if Howard Johnson is your real name.

Since other people have the same exclusive right to a trade name as you have, you cannot use a trade name already in use in the county *in the same field.* The county clerk will have no objection, however, to the trade name of the Peerless Hardware Store, even if the county already has a Peerless Restaurant.

Registration of trade names insures that people do not infringe upon the rights of others or escape creditors by means of frequent name changes. If our friend Howard Johnson decided to open a shoe store, here's how he would register. His first choice for a trade name might be Johnson's Shoes. He ought, however, to submit three names, since it usually costs no more to submit three than it does one at the clerk's office. If Choice A is already in use, he may decide to use Choice B, Howard's Shoes, which is available. The trade name (sometimes referred to otherwise in some states, such as Fictitious Names in Pennsylvania, and known generically as d/b/a, Doing Business As) is used as a business designation. It should also be used as the business checking account designation. Otherwise, despite the trade name, you are still trading as a sole proprietor, not a corporate entity: Howard Johnson, d/b/a Howard's Shoes.

TYPES OF BUSINESS DESIGNATIONS

Being a Sole Proprietor

Trading as a sole proprietor is the least cumbersome way to go into business but, of course, it has its disadvantages. Most important, you are personally liable for everything that happens in the business. You would be named in any lawsuit resulting from the operation of your business, and your personal possessions— your car, your savings, your home, the shirt off your back— would be directly at stake.

Another disadvantage: as sole proprietor you cannot transfer your rights to a buyer. Suppose, for example, that the city adopts an ordinance prohibiting a delicatessen from selling beer and wine. Your delicatessen is protected by a grandfather clause; you may continue to sell beer and wine because you were already selling it before the ordinance was adopted. You cannot, however, transfer your grandfather rights to a new owner; the right begins and ends with you. If your business were operated as a corporation, however, the right would belong to the corporation and could be transferred to the buyer.

Partnerships

A partnership is in effect a collection of proprietors. The partners are each expected to bring something to the enterprise in capital and talent and neither their offerings nor their share of the income have to be equal. This and all other aspects of the partnership ought to be formalized through a legal, written document that spells out the terms of the agreement. All the risks are shared among the partners, and each partner is completely responsible for the actions of his partners and for the enterprise. Although each is personally liable for all debts and judgments involving the business, a creditor may in fact ignore all other partners and concentrate on a particular partner for collection purposes. The partner's only recourse in such a case is to settle with his partners amicably or bring suit against them.

A limited partnership includes partners with a somewhat different relationship. Full partners are called general partners. The limited partners have no management rights over the enterprise but cannot lose more money than they have invested in it—that is, they cannot be liable beyond their investment. A limited partner in a sense is just an investor in the enterprise.

Partnerships, whether general or limited, are not taxed (nor are businesses run under a trade name). The partnership instead files an annual information return (Form 1065) with the IRS. Each partner includes his share of the income on his Schedule E and if the income is subject to Social Security tax, he would also file a Schedule SE. If the partnership lost money in a given year, the loss may be used on Schedule E to offset other income of a similar type.

Corporations

When you set up a corporation, you have established an entity entirely separate from yourself, with its own legal rights, obligations, and liabilities.

The stockholders own a corporation, the board of directors governs it, and its officers manage it. In a small corporation, the stockholders, directors, and officers are usually the same people.

Incorporation is a function of the state government. In most states corporations are in the charge of the secretary of state. This title varies in some states—in Virginia, for example, the agency is called the State Corporation Commission, and in Michigan it is called the Department of Commerce, Corporation Division.

These offices are in effect the same as the Secretariat of State in most states. If the corporation does business in a state other than the one in which it is incorporated, it must file with the proper agency (usually the secretary of state) in that state as a foreign corporation, must pay a fee, and must appoint an agent in that state to be contacted for any legal documents that might be served upon the corporation.

The corporation is required to meet periodically, to keep minutes of its proceedings, and to send annual reports to the state agency and its stockholders. It must keep its own account books and records, and the personal assets of the owners/managers must not be mixed with the corporate assets.

Subchapter S

A separate kind of corporation called Subchapter S is another available option. Many businesspeople like it because it combines some of the advantages of a corporation and of a partnership. The income goes directly to the stockholders/partners and the corporation is not taxed, although it must file information material with the IRS as does a partnership. Subchapter S-type corporations cannot be used for certain purposes, such as real estate ownership.

As a company grows the advantages of a corporation begin to become overwhelming. The days of big partnerships, à la J. P. Morgan, are over. When you have a number of people working for you, considerable assets in capital equipment, large inventories, and when you have acquired a bookkeeping operation to handle the increasing flow of paper, becoming a corporation becomes painless and natural. Your own medical insurance and other work-related coverage can then be completely deducted as corporate expenses, while as a sole proprietor you are allowed to offset only a portion of these expenses as an adjustment on your tax return. You may also be able to effect a savings by obtaining group insurance.

The corporation is also handy as a place to keep money. If your company makes $40,000 in a year, you can pay yourself $20,000 in salary and pay taxes in a rather low bracket while reinvesting the other $20,000 in your own enterprise at little or no taxes. The investment, however, must be genuine; a corporation cannot be used as a personal holding company to keep money from Uncle Sam.

People sometimes tell me that they have taken out a big loan but say "I'm okay because the corporation borrowed the money, not me, and I'm not liable." Knowing that many banks are not going to lend money to your corporation unless a personal guarantee is signed, I usually ask the caller if he has signed such a guarantee, and it usually turns out that he has. In that case he is liable. A bank can go after your assets if you have signed a personal guarantee, and often won't lend you the money any other way.

One last tip. Whenever you form a corporation, make the charter as broad as possible. It doesn't cost anything more for the lawyer's fee. You can create a corporation that can do almost anything—sell wholesale, sell retail, mail-order—that you can think of in the most general terms. Then, if something occurs that causes you to change your mind about your original business purpose, your corporation can easily be used for another purpose.

We did that on several occasions. I had a corporation formed to start the movie theater, and when that deal fell through, I still had the corporation. I continued to pay the annual renewal fee and to keep a registered agent, neither of which cost much, especially when you consider that it costs money to dissolve the corporation anyway. Later, when I started running another business, I just hauled out the old corporation and used it for this entirely different business. You should not, however, use a corporation actively for a number of years and then convert it to another business.

If you buy an existing business it's usually best to form a new corporation and transfer the assets from the former owner's corporation into your new corporation. In that way you avoid hidden liabilities that you didn't know anything about.

ONWARD

In these opening chapters I have tried to mention the major concerns, as I have seen them, that you ought to address at the very outset of your business, and from that we will be going into the day-to-day operation of a business. But as you can see, such hard-and-fast designations don't completely work. Being in the business will teach you a great deal, if you keep your ears open and regard it as on-the-job training. You'll learn things that only come from being on the scene. I can tell you a few from my own experience.

Don't Be Cheap

I was at dinner with some executives at a famous restaurant—one to which I bring important clients regularly. The fellow I was with did not tip the maitre d', did not tip the captain, and the tip he left for the waiter was disgraceful. Fortunately he led the way out, and as I got to the captain I asked: "Did he take care of you?" The captain shook his head. So I tipped him.

The next time I dine at that restaurant, I'll get the table I want. Otherwise I wouldn't even get a reservation, or I'd get a table in the kitchen. That doesn't impress people much when you've got an important meeting.

I'm sure the cheap tipper was pleased that he got off so easily. That's a false economy, though. It pays to take care of people who take care of you. Then when you call, you get reservations, and the table you want, and you walk in and sit down when others wait in line. Even in the smallest of businesses, that is important.

Doing Favors and Remembering

Some people think you're trying to bribe them if you offer them a drink. But send their kid a present, and that's a different story.

Sometimes you have to make something up. Like this: "You mentioned that your son is really interested in chemistry. A friend of mine is manufacturing these chemistry sets. We'd like your son to try it and tell us how he likes it. We want to know his reaction."

Actually you bought the set at the toy discount store, and you don't know anybody who's marketing kids' chemistry sets. But you're a great guy because you recognized that this fellow's son is a budding genius.

If you sent him a case of Scotch, he'd send it back—that would be unethical.

Remembering the names of kids is important. I know guys who keep card files with family information. You ask by name about the kids. You didn't remember their names five minutes earlier, until you looked in the index file. Very important.

When I go to dinner, my first stop, after the first couple of minutes, is the men's room. There I write down all the names of the others at the table so I can remember everybody—Harriet and Joe, Emily and Tom, and so on.

A Voided Check

Some years ago three representatives of a utility company came to see me in connection with hooking up one of my new businesses and becoming a utility customer. They informed me that the utility wanted $1,000 up front as a deposit. It was the company's policy, they told me, to have a good-sized deposit down for a commercial operation.

"Okay," I said, "if that's your policy, I'll give you your deposit." I got out my checkbook and poised the pen over it. "I'm wondering, though," I added, "what kind of interest you're going to pay me on my money."

The three representatives told me that the company would pay me 5 percent interest—a rate, I was informed, that was allowed by the state's Public Utility Commission.

I filled out the check and handed it to them. "I see in the newspaper that your utility is paying eleven percent interest to your bondholders," I said. "Yet you're coming to me and forcing me to lend you money at five percent after you've acknowledged publicly that money costs you eleven percent. Now I don't want to be Don Quixote and I have no interest in tilting at windmills. But if you're going to shortchange me that way, I can assure you that I'll start an action, go to the courts, and ask that every depositor is paid the same interest rate that you're paying your bondholders. I suspect that if I prevail in the courts—and I think the argument is fairly reasonable—it's going to cost you a lot of money."

The three of them looked at each other and, after a short silence, one of them said: "Mr. Williams, why don't you forget about that check? I really see no reason why someone with your outstanding credit standing should have to pay a deposit at all." They left almost immediately, and I wrote "Void" across the check and threw it away.

I needed that money for my own business, and my move saved it from going into the hands of someone else. It isn't something I learned in school, or anything I've ever read in a book about small business. It came from experience on the street.

Failure

If you want to know about failure, ask me. I've been there several times. Some of my early adventures seem to have the theme of failure running through them. I worked at a Newark insurance agency and found I should have taken disaster insurance. Then I tried selling fire extinguishers and soon found my job extinguished as well. Of course I was only eighteen years old then.

Then a partner and I decided to start a restaurant. The building had formerly housed a drugstore in which I had worked as a kid. The bottles that we tossed in the garbage—apothecary bottles with etched lettering in the front—were probably worth a fortune. I remember hurling a huge mortar and pestle away—if I had held on to this stuff, it would have made me rich. But we couldn't wait to throw it out.

My partner and I were kids just out of the military service. We borrowed money from the bank on the strength of nothing but our enthusiasm, and opened the only air-conditioned restaurant in the area. We lost our shirts. We knew nothing about pricing, or buying, or running daily specials. Most important, we knew absolutely nothing about the hiring and training of employees. We thought somebody walked through the door and you stuck him on the job. On the opening day the ice cream company brought a couple of specialists in. We figured that they would run the place that day. But that didn't help us on the second day.

No failure could have been more total. Yet out of that failure something came. At least we managed to sell it, so maybe we were better salesmen than we were retailers. Because I had a bit of experience with running a restaurant, the college I went to later—I was only a sophomore but fairly mature, in my late twenties—made me director of the Student Union Building, and gave me faculty status. I made a success out of that operation.

Maybe you have to fail a few times before you succeed. Successful people fail more often than unsuccessful people, because they try more things.

7

The Seven Mules: Part I

Before the heyday of professional football, college football was avidly followed all over America as a major sport. And the greatest team of the early 1920s was Notre Dame. In 1924 everybody was talking about the Four Horsemen—the name that sportswriter Grantland Rice had popularized in his columns about the famous Notre Dame backfield.

The members of the backfield were getting so much publicity, and beginning to take it so seriously, that Knute Rockne, the team's coach, thought it was important to bring them down a few pegs. One Saturday as Notre Dame made ready to take the field for the opening kickoff, Rockne decided to keep his stellar linemen, who were called the Seven Mules, on the bench and put in the college's second-string line.

The Four Horsemen didn't do much galloping in the early minutes of that game. Every time the ball was snapped back, the opposing team threw the ball carrier for a loss. Eventually Rockne took pity on his bedraggled and reeling backfield and sent in the Seven Mules.

As the center, who was team captain, entered the huddle, he said: "What seems to be the matter, boys? It seems you need a little help." With the first team back in action, Notre Dame began to click, rolled over its opposition, and went on to an undefeated season.

09

The Four Horsemen were unquestionably good football players, but not so great that they didn't need a lot of help. The same is true for any entrepreneur, no matter how good a broken-field runner he (or she) may be. Unless you have a solid line in front of you, protecting you from onrushing disasters, you are not going to score any touchdowns. No matter how independent you think you have become by going into business for yourself, you are going to need your equivalent of the Seven Mules—your banker, your lawyer, your insurance agent, your accountant, your politicians, your employees, and your family.

You have to shop for a bank and for a banker, and not just open an account in the one down the street because it's convenient. Twenty-five years ago a million-dollar customer was an important person when he or she walked into a bank; now a million-dollar customer (someone who passes a million dollars through a bank in the course of a year) is just a minnow in the sea of banking. You need to find a bank where you'll be a valued customer.

As for a lawyer, naturally you're looking for talent, but perhaps more important, I find that one of the commonest mistakes of small business people is trying to get along without one. Even a mediocre lawyer is better than none at all.

You should be looking for an insurance agent who wants and needs your business, not somebody who is comfortable and complacent.

In all three cases, you should be looking for somebody who is interested in *you*, and that's not always easy to find. Let's expand on these three important members of your line and on what they can do for you.

YOUR BANKER

If you walk into the lobby of the headquarters of a major bank, you'll have to be a big shot to be recognized; with the kind of money you represent, you're just a number. But if you do your banking at a small branch of a big bank, you'll be greeted when you walk in, because you'll be important. That is the place to put your accounts. The new managers learning the business are there, and they want to impress you. You can use this to your advantage.

Being Known to Your Banker

Let your banker know who you are immediately. The branch manager should know enough about you so that if you use him or her as a credit reference, the recognition is immediate. And you should know the branch manager's name, so that if you are looking for credit at Enterprise Associates, you can offhandedly say, "Call Joan Jones at the East Willow Branch of the First National Bank." And give them the telephone number. Now obviously you are somebody who does business with the bank so often that you know the telephone number.

Even more important is the reaction that the bank gives to the inquiry when the company where you are seeking credit calls.

"Hello, this is Tom Smith at Enterprise Associates. Bruce Williams used you as a reference."

"Oh, yes, Mr. Williams has been banking here for twenty years."

Right off the top of her head, Joan Jones recognizes your name. She doesn't have to say, "Hold it for a moment and we'll take a look at the computer."

I recently applied for two lines of credit in the same week, and they were both approved in a matter of two hours. Credit can be established, but it has to be cultivated, watered, and manured. You do that by knowing your banker.

One night when I was having dinner with a very famous radio personality, I asked him what restaurant in New York he liked best. He said, "The one I'm best-known in." That's true for banking as well. It may sound presumptuous and egotistical, but it's not just to flatter your ego—it's to help your business. And it's up to you to make them know that you're important.

When your little bank changes managers, go in and talk to the new manager. Begin by giving him the One Commandment: Thou shalt not bounce any of my checks. Make it clear that if he does so, he will lose all of your accounts immediately. When those bad checks are listed in the morning, you want to make certain he has not put any of yours on the list. Tell the bank manager: "Call me. Tell me the problem, and I'll tell you where to switch the money from, or I'll be there with the money in a few hours."

You won't have that kind of clout at a big bank. The big bank will tell you that a senior officer must approve the honoring of an overdrawn check. Such a matter goes before a series of people, and it's virtually impossible for you to influence the outcome. At a small branch, though, every overdrawn check just goes to the manager's desk for a decision. You can influence his decision because for his little branch, which lacks big commercial depositors, yours is a fairly important account. If your accounts turn over a half-million dollars a year, you're a substantial depositor to him, and will be treated that way. Make it a point, without being overbearing, to ensure that the branch manager knows how important you are to him. Play him like a violin.

When I failed to make a loan payment recently—the coupon had not been sent to me—the bank withdrew the payment from my checking account. I called the bank to say that I had not given permission to do any such thing. I reminded the bank manager that I had a lot of money going through the bank every year and that I could take it elsewhere—and then go to the bank president and tell him why. Don't let the bank intimidate you.

I want to do business in a bank where the managers have authority. Some banks give the branch manager authority to buy a few postage stamps, and that's all. He or she has to call the central office for any bigger decision. That, too, is not to your interest, because you don't mean that much to the people in the central office. Find out from the manager how much autonomy he or she has. What level of loan can be approved in the office? Can an overdraft be handled in the office? And how much is needed to go beyond immediate autonomy—a simple telephone call, or a board of directors meeting?

The problem of being nothing more than a number to a bank has increased recently because of the liberalized laws governing banking. Not too many years ago banks were not allowed to do any interstate banking, and in many states they could only operate in a single county. In some cases they couldn't even leave the city. So there were a lot of little banks, and if you were a merchant you were a big customer.

Then came the change. The argument was that the little banks could never compete with the big banks because of the lending restrictions. In a bank that is part of the federal system, not more than 10 percent of the assets can be lent to a single lender. This meant that if General Motors wanted to build a new plant it had to go to twenty banks, or one huge bank. The argument was that the little banks could merge and compete with the big ones.

From the point of view of the stockholder, and the bank, it's a valid argument, but it does not work in favor of the little guy. More than ever, he counts for naught in the banking world. One of the major banks tried to institute a rule that you couldn't talk to a teller unless you had $20,000 in the bank. You had to deal with a machine. The bank didn't have time for you. Well, the small depositors were ready to tear the bank down, and the bank management backed off. But that's the direction banking is taking.

A Bank for Your Needs

Check on whether your bank is competitive in what it offers. If you're in business, it's likely that you will need more than one bank. One of my accounts is in a large commercial bank. They're competitive for corporate loans, but not for mortgages. Frequently it's necessary to have two or three banks.

Even if you are opening just a simple checking account there are all sorts of options. Find the one that's for you. Honoring overdrafts, as I have already indicated, is a major consideration, not even an option but a necessity. Some banks have an overdraft credit line. But some banks charge a nickel for each check, more for each foreign check. Another bank will have a $1 flat monthly rate for all foreign checks. If you're depositing five hundred checks a month, five hundred nickels is a lot more than twenty nickels.

If you go to four banks in the same trade area about opening a commercial account, you will find that the charges vary widely. Some charge flat fees, some have a charge for each transaction. One may charge you for your checks, another may give them to you at no charge. A third may give you a big break on charges if you order thousands of checks at a time.

Many banks don't give any interest on corporate checking accounts. However, there is nothing to prevent you from cutting a deal whereby the money goes into the money market in the bank and you can transfer it to your checking by telephone. So you can deposit your money in the money fund account, where it is drawing interest, and transfer it when you need it.

Now that the rules are relaxed the bank can make almost any kind of a deal. This puts a higher value on your bargaining ability and your knowhow. If you don't know what is going on, you will be taken. Maybe not deliberately, but because the bank officers don't know all the subtleties. If you have a cash flow going through a bank you should find a way to do something with it, even if it doesn't stay there long. A fellow with a gas station can easily run a million dollars through a bank in a year, and that means that at any particular time he has $20,000 in the account. To have it there earning no interest makes no sense. There are little subenterprises in your own enterprise, and one of these is banking and how to get maximum effect out of your money.

Goodbye to the Float

This has become necessary because the old days when you had a float to play with are gone. Electronic banking has virtually eliminated the float. It used to be that you could write a check and figure that you had a couple of days before it was cashed. Now there's no way to tell.

There were some abuses of the float in the past. An artful floater would pay an Eastern company with a check from a San Francisco bank and pay a Los Angeles company with a New York bank check. More recently the abuse was going in the other direction. The banks took up to fourteen days in some cases to credit money to your account that they could actually clear in twelve hours. So they were getting the float; they had the use of your money, interest-free, before they credited it to you. Recent federal and state legislation has limited the float to two days for a check on a local bank and five days for one from a more distant bank, in most cases.

Homeowner's Line of Credit

One of the new deals that has opened up in the volatile world of banking is a homeowner's line of credit. This can be extremely useful to a small business. The idea of a line of credit, to which I have alluded earlier, is that you need the money when you need it—you don't have time to sit around waiting for a loan to be approved.

Say a merchant comes along and offers you a truckload of computer paper at 20 cents on the dollar. Your business uses a lot of computer paper, and this is a great buy. But he needs the cash up front—he needs the money fast, and that's why he's offering such a great deal.

These kinds of buys come along in business all the time. I

know of one large corporation that keeps one month's cash on hand at all times. Now that's liquidity. So if a supplier is overstocked or needs cash, the company can save a bundle. But the average little guy has a difficult time coming up with big money in a hurry.

The homeowner's line of credit, which is available in most states, is the answer to a little guy's prayer. Here's how it works. You apply in advance for what is essentially a second mortgage on your house, based on how much equity you have in it. If you have a house worth $100,000, and the principal left on your mortgage is only $30,000, you have $70,000 in equity in your house. Based on that, the bank might give you as much as a $60,000 line of credit. It's pre-approved. In some banks there is an application charge, but if you wait until they have a sale, the bank will probably waive the charge.

There are psychological advantages to this method as well. You have applied for the credit under ideal conditions. You're relaxed, you don't need the money, your business is going well. The loan is in place. All you have to do is write a check and the money will be there. Suppose you went for this same loan at another time: you have a tremendous buy possible on computer paper but you don't have the money because your biggest customer is behind in his payments. You go to the bank and ask for a loan, and the bank officer thinks, well, this fellow has a cash-flow problem—maybe we had better look at this proposal a little more carefully. So he or she says, "Let me take this to the board." Meanwhile your desperation grows.

But with the homeowner's line of credit there is no desperation because you applied when you didn't need the money. It's a really good system for you. And the interest rates, pegged to the prime rate, are not bad.

Business Accounts Are Different

If your previous experience with banks has only been in

personal checking and savings accounts, you will find that commercial accounts by and large entail more charges. They all charge more for commercial accounts because they have agreed among themselves to do so. But if you try to get by using your own personal checking account you will have problems, unless the business is just your name. Otherwise you will have trouble putting the checks in the bank. If your business is incorporated, and you put the checks into your personal checking account, technically you are defrauding the corporation, although it's unlikely that the IRS would care.

Of course, if you're really operating on a shoestring it might pay to get a personal account for your business. The bank isn't going to like it, however, and you won't be one of those favored customers—a status that may be important for you.

YOUR LAWYER

The number of people who try to get through business transactions without using a lawyer never ceases to amaze me. Many of them end up in some kind of trouble—which is where I usually pick up the story. This trouble in most cases could have been avoided by engaging a lawyer, and would have cost less money.

To cite one recent example: a man purchased a vacant lot without being represented by a lawyer, then discovered that he could not build on it. In order to get a building permit, he needed permission to install a septic tank or some kind of self-contained disposal system, since the area had no sewer lines. To get that permission, to show that the ground could take a septic system, that sanitation problems would not develop from leakage into the soil, he needed a percolation test. He had never heard of a percolation test, but when the test failed he became extremely familiar with the subject. The man could not understand why he could not take the lot back to the seller and get his money back.

The seller, however, had made no representation that a building could be constructed on this lot—although the purchaser may have thought such a representation was implied.

Any youngster in law school could have protected him from this misstep. This is a rather unsophisticated example, but something more complicated can come up in business transactions that a highly sophisticated layperson might miss and a lawyer would catch immediately.

It's best to get an attorney *before* you need one. Get out and meet a lawyer. You can tell him that you have no need for him now but would like to get acquainted with him and find out a little about how he thinks. Then when the time comes that you do need a lawyer, you can pick up the telephone and call him, and he already knows you.

I never consider any serious transaction involving property without being represented by an attorney. Then if something goes wrong, I have somebody to account to me for the mistake. Say there is an easement across the back of the property. That might not wash out your purchase, but you should be aware of it, and a lawyer is more likely to spot such matters than you are. People can buy property with a whole batch of covenants of which they are unaware unless a lawyer represents them.

You have to trust your lawyer. You may have to tell him that you've done something illegal, that you've been stealing, that you're cheating the government. You may have to tell him that you had five drinks and were at fault in the accident. These revelations are not supposed to go any further.

Competency is important in a lawyer, but an awareness of his or her own shortcomings is important too. The intelligent lawyer should be able to say forthrightly: this is not my area, let me recommend another lawyer for this. The scope of the law is ever-broadening and few lawyers today can master every facet of every kind of law. Nevertheless, for a beginning business a general practice lawyer is probably best.

You probably will need a lawyer as registered agent if you have incorporated your business. This provides someone on whom legal papers can be served and the like. This service does not cost much. And if you do incorporate, you ought to have a lawyer do it for you. You can do it without an attorney, but in my estimation it's not wise. Many of your corporate records will be kept in the lawyer's office.

If you have to appear before the governing body of a municipality, it's foolish to choose a lawyer active in the "out" party to represent you. The party of influence is the right party to go with on such occasions. I'm still waiting to see the first governing body that's completely unsullied by politics; its members got there by paying their political dues and it's realistic to assume that they stay there the same way. It's not dishonest for you to take cognizance of that—it's smart.

YOUR INSURANCE AGENT

Let's start with some clarification. When we talk about insurance in connection with your business, we're basically discussing commercial business insurance. If you have employees, we may also be talking about health and accident coverage and worker compensation insurance.

Commercial business insurance is basically of two kinds: property, or first-party insurance, and casualty, or third-party insurance. The latter is often called liability insurance.

Property Insurance
Property insurance covers your possessions. If you own the building in which your business is located, you should have property coverage for it. The insurance can cover the building's actual value or its replacement value. For example, you may be operating in an old building worth no more than $30,000, but if it were to be destroyed, you might not be able to find a similar

building for under $200,000. So you might want replacement coverage, which would of course cost more in premiums than actual value coverage. Other property coverage insures your inventory, your goods while in transit, your trucks, and so on. If you deal in goods, you might also need these kinds of coverage.

Liability Insurance

Most people tend to concentrate too heavily on property insurance and underestimate the exposures involved in liability. "If that building burns down," the businessperson reasons, "I'd lose $50,000 in property and inventory, but why do I need a lot of liability coverage? I can't get in that kind of a jam." So he takes out $50,000 in liability coverage, which is completely inadequate.

People who think this way have no idea what is happening in the American civil courts. The public has taken up the Deep Pockets view of litigation—that when somebody has been maimed the compensation should be huge and somebody must be tapped to pay for it. This is only right where real negligence is involved; but some juries have gone overboard in fixing blame. With a taste for the fantastic, the juries have awarded damages in the millions.

You may think you are exempt from this phenomenon because you're just running a little stall in a flea market, selling sandals. Somebody buys a pair of your sandals. Later he stumbles, lands on his head, suffers brain damage to the extent that he can never work again, and sues you (as well as the manufacturer) for selling him deficient goods. The jury faces a dilemma: this man is truly incapacitated and somebody has to support him. You may be that somebody.

Take another example. You make dresses. Now, how can *that* get you in any trouble? A little boy swallows a button from his mother's dress, and you are sued because twenty witnesses claim he has been permanently damaged because you failed to sew enough threads through the button and should have made it stronger. This may be ridiculous—and the jury may think so too—but are you aware of how much it will cost you to defend yourself? And that your lawyer may suggest a settlement rather than paying for the enormous costs of a full trial and a possible appeal?

That's why I carry $4 million worth of liability coverage for a truck that I have on the road. If a shop burns down, all I lose is the value of the property and inventory, but if that truck runs into a school bus, there's no limit on the damage it can do. All your assets could disappear in such a horrible catastrophe.

What Kind of Agent?

The person who handles your insurance ought to be looking out for your interests. That's why an independent insurance agent, who represents a variety of companies, can work better for you than can an exclusive agent, who is held captive to a single company. Even if the captive agent works for a low-priced insurance company, the cheapest insurance is not always the best. In insurance you usually get only what you pay for. The independent agent is able to search through several policies of various companies he represents to find one that has the kind of insurance best suited to your needs.

A lot of insurance agents are guys in their late forties or early fifties who have paid their dues, worked hard, gone out nights to see clients, and now have begun to reap the rewards of years of hard work. Their book is full, the telephone keeps ringing, the contacts keep working. Good for them; they probably deserve their success. That, however, is not the kind of agent I'm looking for. If you have this kind of an agent and he provides good service, I'm not saying you should abandon him. But my preference is for a younger, hungrier, hustling fellow who really needs my business.

When I look at life insurance, I'm interested in the lowest price. After the funeral is over, the insurance company can't come to the survivors and offer $800,000 for my $1 million policy on the grounds that I was pretty much worn out anyway.

On casualty and property policies, however, price is only one factor to consider. If the store burns down, you want somebody on your side—your insurance agent. If a serious dispute arises about the value of destroyed merchandise, your agent, if he is a decent producer for the company, is a valuable ally.

Some people like to shop around for their commercial insurance. I'd rather put everything in the hands of a single agent. I'm not impressed that I can save a little money on fire coverage by placing it here, and save a little on worker's compensation by placing it there. I end up with five insurance agents, each of them making a little on my premiums, but I'm nothing much of a customer to any of them. I'm very dispensable. If I have all my coverage with one agent, I'm important to him: a big customer. If I call with a problem, he'll skip lunch to work it out for me. As one of his big customers, you may also get a number of free services that otherwise you would be charged for. He might even take you to lunch.

A broker should review your insurance annually. If he doesn't, that ought to be a warning signal. The limits on liability that are appropriate one year may have to be adjusted the following year. Because of the replacement value of your real estate, for example, it's important that the policy be brought up to date regularly.

Most insurance companies operate with real property on an 80 percent factor. That is, if you don't carry coverage for at least 80 percent of the building's worth, you become a co-insurer with them in the loss and will not be paid in full. Sometimes this is not such a bad idea. If you have a building for which a total loss seems almost impossible, you may be able to bring down the premium. Your agent ought to advise you on such matters, but a lot of agents don't.

If an agent sells you collision insurance on old automobiles that should not be covered, in my opinion he has disqualified himself from serious consideration. He sold you something that any informed person knows you do not need. Even if you asked him for it, he should have convinced you otherwise, because his relationship to you should be that of an adviser.

Here's a tip of the sort your agent ought to give you: if you want to drop coverage on an insurance policy, don't cancel it. Suspend it. You'll get a cash savings. Frequently if you cancel a policy in mid-term you get short-rated, which means it will cost extra money. Often if you suspend it, you'll be pro-rated, which will cost you nothing extra.

YOUR ACCOUNTANT

Don't think that you can get by without an accountant; that's another of those false economies that will cost you more in the end.

If, however, you have a bent for figures, you can do a lot of the record-keeping yourself. That doesn't mean that you won't need an accountant. The accountant will set up your record-keeping system for you, so that a bookkeeper (who might be you) can make the daily entries. Bookkeeping is a good skill for one of your children to learn: you can write off his or her wages, and the child probably will not have to pay taxes on it.

Many business people who unhesitatingly ask questions of their lawyer or insurance agent hesitate to question their accountant, as if not understanding figures is "dumb." You should be neither in awe nor in a state of supposed mental inferiority to your accountant. He or she should be able to explain methods and procedures to you in terms that you are able to understand. Some accountants enjoy making their clients feel inadequate; one of these should not be your accountant.

Your accountant's work should be reviewed regularly. Changing accountants is painful because it means someone else has to become familiar with your books, but an accountant interested in getting the work will probably give you a free initial consultation. If you hear the views of an accountant whose ideas and procedures vary from those of your present accountant, that does not mean you should drop the one you have, but you ought to inquire about these differing views with your present accountant.

It is helpful to have an accountant who understands your business, and industry specialization in accounting is a growing trend. "Creative accounting" has become a buzzword in contemporary business, but with the modest dimensions of your business, the wilder creations of accounting will not come into play. Even in a small business, however, an accountant should be working up new ways of doing things, ways that will save you money and cut your taxes. Just because you don't have any problems with the IRS, incidentally, does not mean that your accountant is doing a good job.

If you can afford to meet more often than quarterly with your accountant, it may be worthwhile to do so. If your business increases or declines, reacts to a growing or a contracting economy, the changes that result can affect everything from your cash on hand to your estimated taxes, and an accountant should be following and adjusting to the changes. A good measure of whether to have these more frequent meetings is to try them and see whether they pay for themselves in savings. That is, for that matter, the criterion of a good accountant: he should pay for himself by recommending ways of saving money, and that includes ways of saving on his own services.

Records are not only essential for your business, but a

requirement of the government. Later we'll examine record-keeping and will have more to say about accountants.

THE POLITICIANS

When I speak of the politician as one of your Seven Mules, I'm referring to everybody in the whole political structure, from the local zoning officer on up to members of Congress and the president, but basically local government has the largest immediate impact on business enterprise.

The business climate in the city, town, or village in which you operate has a crucial effect on your success or failure. This climate can be determined before you locate your business, if you ask questions of local businesspeople about what kind of attitudes the local officials display.

Most city fathers (and mothers) want to welcome business. They seek business and industry because shopping centers, factories, and office buildings provide a solid tax base on one side of the ledger, without adding children to the town's population on the other side. From a taxation point of view, residential development is less desirable than business development because it brings more children, which adds to the largest single cost for local government: the public schools. Nonresidential growth profits a town, contributing more in taxes than it demands in services, while residential growth demands more in services than it contributes in taxes. And nonresidential growth creates jobs, which further increases the tax base.

In many towns with political savvy, the political parties observe a tacit agreement that they will fight about almost anything else, but that business and industry should be beyond the reach of partisan wrangling. In some towns, however, the agreement does not hold, the bipartisan business climate evaporates, and everything becomes fair game. This hurts business.

Also bad for business: overly zealous officials who want to

show the world how incorruptible they are and come out with a tape measure to check out your sign, then force you to remove it if it's a half-inch too large.

Incidentally, the right party for you to belong to is the party in power. Keep up your lines of communication with the Democrats and the Republicans and contribute to both parties.

Most beginners in business are unaware of the large role that local politics plays in helping or retarding their success. I'm going to have a lot more to say about it in a forthcoming chapter.

8

The Seven Mules: Part II

EMPLOYEES

Employees. They can make or break your organization.

Hiring

I've done a lot of hiring in my time. About 90 percent of the hiring interview is over before the applicant sits down. As he or she walked through the door—the dress, the walk, the look, all contributed to an instant impression. If it's a negative impression, that's difficult to overcome. I tend to make quick decisions on hiring. I make some mistakes, but so do people who take a month to decide, and I'm not unhappy with my batting average.

I look for curiosity in people. Incurious people just do their job, and they don't want to know any more about the business than the part that their job involves. "I just work here" is their motto; they never look at the broader picture, which severely limits their development. Curious people ask questions and learn about the business, gradually becoming ready to take on more responsibility.

One of the applicants for a summer counseling job at my camp some years back was a young woman who showed up with her Water Safety Instructor certificate in swimming. I explained to her that everybody doubled in brass at my camp and that I needed a swimming instructor who could also drive a van with a stick shift. I asked if she could do it.

"No," she said, "but I'll be able to drive one tomorrow morning."

I hired her that minute. She was ready to adjust; she was willing to learn how to use a stick shift that very evening; and apparently she wanted the job badly. As it turned out she did a marvelous job as a counselor and returned to work for me again in subsequent summers. In jobs like these, most of the people who walk through the door have the qualifications—that is, they can drive and have a water safety instructor certificate. Their names and faces become a blur; so it's often a little extra something—an extra willingness, a sign of confidence—that gets them the job.

I'm looking for flexibility. I don't want to hire somebody who seems rigid, such as the fellow who can't come in at six for the interview because that's the dinner hour. Or the woman who'll only work certain hours because she must be home when her husband gets home and must be home when her son gets back from school. I applaud her devotion to her husband and son but I don't think I have a place for her.

Big companies have strict hiring policies that mean nothing to a little operation, such as not hiring older people. That's largely the government's fault. A big company is practically prohibited from hiring a qualified sixty year old because of the laws governing health coverage and pension plans. It just costs the company too much. The man may be perfectly willing to waive such fringe benefits, but the company isn't allowed to accept his waiver. In a little business, in which you don't have all those perquisites anyway, you can hire older people, and should. I have hired people in their eighties, and I had an eighty-year-old man working for me at the time I was writing this book. I hired a seventy-five-year-old woman as a teacher at the nursery school, and she ran rings around the younger ones. Some people are old at thirty and others still young at seventy. Some people are responsible at twenty and others still irresponsible at fifty-five. For a small business, age should not be a consideration in hiring.

Remember that you are hiring for a business, not selecting companions for a cruise. I've heard people say, "I wouldn't hire that son of a gun." The reason? "I don't like him." That's not a valid reason. You're hiring talent, not expressing all your likes and dislikes. I've hired people I did not like, and I respected their ability even if I didn't like them personally. That takes maturity.

One of the best sources of new employees, incidentally, is your present employees. First, because they recognize that they are going to accept some responsibility for the recommendation and are not likely to recommend a washout; secondly, because they know that they are going to have to work with that person, and it's to their interest for the worker to be effective.

This flies in the face of corporate wisdom, but I have no trouble with nepotism. If one of my employees has a worthy brother, sister, mother, aunt, or cousin, I'm ready to give him or her a shot at a job. We have been very fortunate over the years with families. It's created a problem with the payroll—it's full of identical last names—but that's the only difficulty I've noticed. (In one case three members of the same family working for us all have the same initial in their first names, which has been a minor hassle because we use that as an additional identification if the last names are the same.)

Big companies don't like a situation in which a husband may be supervising his wife, or vice versa. They also think that too many people in the family may create conspiracies—one is in accounting, another in accounts payable, and who knows but that they may break new ground in creative embezzlement? I can understand these quibbles. In a small operation, however, the problem should not exist, because you should be on top of things. Good people are hard enough to find without arbitrarily eliminating one because she's the sister of someone who is working for you.

What I Want

Since you see them all the time and you can see what they are producing, the assessment of employees is much easier in a small business.

Some people have to be told everything. If there is spilled coffee on the floor, they will step over it until somebody tells them to get rid of it. This does not mean, however, that they are not good employees; it just means that they continuously have to be told what to do. Others will take the initiative. If they see that the floor needs sweeping, they'll get a broom and do it. If they see fingerprints on a windowpane, they'll wipe them clean.

I expect my employees to be on time. I don't ask them to be two minutes early but it irks me when they are five minutes late. I see some significance in it, as well as in behavior at quitting time. Can you set your watch by the moment their buns are out the door? They have the right to leave on the dot, but as an employer it will hardly thrill you to watch them lining up to rush out when the hour strikes. If events are moving slowly, let your employees leave fifteen minutes early. You can then hope, although the hope may not be fulfilled, that they will someday stay fifteen minutes late when they are needed.

Your business will have key employees, people you want to encourage to stay with you. The problem is that you won't know who they are when you hire them. You discover that over the course of time. A person who gets the Big Picture, who is company-oriented, who puts in extra effort—that's the key person.

Some employers think the smart way to treat employees is to badger them and browbeat them to squeeze the most productivity out of them for the least money. I think this is shortsighted and poor business. Treat your employees well and pay them

130

well, especially the key people. If they are doing a good job, give them a bonus—and praise them as well. Sometimes a clap on the shoulder is more appreciated than money. If you browbeat them, you'll get surface respect, but they'll find a way to get even. Believe it.

Make your employees feel that they are part of the organization. The Japanese base their whole employment policy on this—they create a lifetime relationship. Of late they have been doing fairly well at it. The allegiance has to go both ways, which means that if you practice it you have to be loyal to your employees as well.

I believe in making the workplace pleasant. Since you and your employees spend so much time there, it's important. Little things are very important to them, like providing a refrigerator so your employees can keep their drinks or their lunches cool. Or providing a microwave oven so they can heat their food, or make popcorn if they wish. It costs little in investment and it makes them happy. Some employers argue that it's stupid to try to please your employees, that they'll just take advantage of you. I've heard those arguments and admit there's some truth in them. I've also known people who practiced the son-of-a-bitch style and did well with it. But I don't like it, and I think it can blow up in your face.

Actually you can come out better monetarily this way as well. Ask most people whether they would rather have a little higher wage or work for a little less in a place where they are happy and appreciated, and 95 percent will say the latter.

The same is true with regard to flexible hours. If you can let your employee work his or her own hours, let it happen. The fact is that you can keep them for less money that way.

I'm paternalistic with my employees. I'll even lend money to keep a good worker. Just recently I signed a note to guarantee the rent for two years to one of my employees because her credit rating was not adequate. At $400 a month that was a pretty fair-sized commitment. I don't think you need to be afraid to trust your employees this far, if you know them well enough.

The Difference They Make

There are some businesses in which employees don't make a lot of difference. If you have a convenience store, for example, you will undoubtedly hire people at the minimum wage, because that's all you will be able to afford, and all you can expect of them is minimum wage performance. The employees will stand behind the counter, ring up the cash register, restock the shelves, and mop the floor. In this kind of operation, probably running twenty-four hours a day, you can expect a revolving door of employees coming on and quitting all the time. Since it is not a career job, people are not going to stay at it, and trying to keep them is probably a waste of time.

But that is the exception, in my view. In most businesses that require a relationship between the customer and the employee, you do not want a quick turnover. If someone calls your place and asks for Angie only to find that she has been replaced by Mary Jane, and six weeks later asks for Mary Jane only to learn that Susan has replaced her, the customer is not filled with a feeling of confidence about your operation. In order to keep these people with you, you have to pay them.

In most businesses, employees are crucial. If you don't have employees you're like a one-man barber shop. No matter how fast your fingers work, you can cut only so many heads of hair, and so you are physically limited. You must have employees because you cannot be everywhere and do everything.

When people work for you, you can still be making money when you are at home with a cold or in traction for four months. You ought to be able to clear enough profit on the work of three or so employees to provide your own salary. True, you may be more talented than your employees, and true, the employees actually make more work because you have to make up payrolls, pay taxes, keep more complicated books, and so on—but to me having employees is what an enterprise is all about. That's the whole capitalistic system—making money on your capital and someone else's labor.

As your business gets bigger, you will need a larger profit margin because of the managerial and supervisory work that develops. You cannot personally supervise thirty or forty people, so you need to designate a worker who helps supervise. Eventually supervising duties will begin to take nearly all of his time. If he makes thirty cents, every one of the thirty people he supervises has to make an extra penny to pay his salary. When your business grows to one hundred employees, you need three supervisors. At that point you probably need a supervisor of supervisors, and the people being supervised need to make a few more cents to pay his salary.

For the time being, however, your business is going to be rather small. And the smaller the business, the more important is each individual employee. If you have a business with two hundred drivers, and one of them is out sick, it doesn't mean that much. You can cover his route by shifting a few drivers. But if you have a business with *two* drivers and one of them is out, half your driving work force is gone. You've got a real problem.

Vacations are a problem, too, in a small operation. A lot of cooperation is required from your people. If you are in a business where you can backlog work, the problem is much easier to handle. Some companies just close down for two weeks and everyone goes on vacation at once. That's impossible for some businesses to do, however. They can't expect their customers to go somewhere else for two weeks and then come back when the vacation is over. Some businesses, especially those dealing in perishables, can't warehouse goods for vacation time.

This is where the flexibility of your employees is important. They have to be ready to help you during vacation time, possibly by working overtime. If possible, show your own flexibility by letting them decide when to work the overtime. If they want to come in early, or work a twelve-hour day, or work weekends, why be rigid about it?

Invest your time and attention in these valuable resources of yours, your employees. Taking them to lunch or to dinner contributes to the operation. It also stimulates a more informal and relaxed conversation that can invite observations that will help the business. People are flattered that what they have to say is important to you, and should know that their views are sought after. But the employer should also be sensitive to his employee's position: going to dinner may be an imposition rather than a favor. A woman with a family at home may have to hire a baby-sitter or rearrange her entire family schedule so as not to disappoint you. In such cases a luncheon or an occasional informal discussion in the office, possibly over coffee and rolls, may work more effectively.

When you have an ineffective employee, you cannot afford to keep him around—not so much because he won't work, although that doesn't help, but because he demoralizes your organization. That's especially true of the small business. In a big business he would just be lost, and you might be able to tolerate him.

I have never had a single instance of trouble with employees because I fired someone. On the contrary, I have had problems with employees asking me to get rid of somebody when I was reluctant to do so. Except when somebody has been caught stealing from you, firing is not something you do with relish, but at times you will have to do it.

Their Value

The employee is in a sense a commodity, like capital or inventory. You can draw an analogy between the pay of an employee and what you can afford to pay in interest.

If I went to the bank and borrowed money at 50 percent interest, it wouldn't bother me a bit as long as I knew that I could get 60 percent with it. But I wouldn't want to pay 3 percent interest if all I could get with it after I borrowed it was 2 percent. What I'm saying is, it's the spread that counts.

The same is true with employees. It's impossible to overpay a salesperson who is on commission. As long as an employee produces more in revenue than what he or she is paid, you have a viable employee.

But people think, understandably, that they are entitled to an increase every so often. In many circumstances, however, they eventually bump into the house limit. They are only producing so much, and you cannot afford to pay them any more. In that case the employer has to be honest with the employee and say, "You've hit your limit."

Some employers have trouble with this. But if an employee comes to them and asks why it is that Jones makes more money than he does, they have to be honest.

Why do you pay an airline pilot more than a bus driver? Both of them transport people, operate a public carrier. But if the two of us grabbed the first five hundred people who walked past, I'll bet I could train more of them to be successful bus drivers than you could train to be successful pilots. That's why airplane pilots are paid more. And that's why Jones makes more money than the unhappy employee—because it's harder to find somebody to do Jones's job.

Now the next question that your unhappy employee and you should discuss is how the employee can make himself more valuable. There's no problem about paying him more money if the value is there.

As a corollary to the thought that you cannot overpay a salesperson who works on straight commission, I must add that a salesperson ought to bear some responsibility for losses. He or she gets a bonus for profitable business and some kind of penalty for unprofitable business. Not to be mean to the employee, but to have a kind of negative incentive.

Suppose your salesperson sells an $80-a-year service contract for a garden tractor and it costs the business thousands of dollars of losses in service costs because the salesman sold a tractor that was too light for the job. That's a big minus and there ought to be some kind of accounting for it.

But beware of disincentives among your employees. If there's no reward for your employees for doing the right thing, but you are hard on your employees for making mistakes, they are going to do the safe thing every time. So reward them for the right decisions because they will not bet their jobs if they have nothing to gain from it.

A common notion among employers is that their employees are getting paid for doing their job, so why should they be rewarded for doing it? That's not good management. A reward, incidentally, does not have to be money every time. A pat on the back is better sometimes.

Perquisites

If you can reward your employee with something besides money, by all means do it. If you pay him or her another dollar, you have to pay even more for social security, unemployment, and worker comp. Your employee has to contribute to some of these funds as well. But if you give a perk, often both you and your employee are better off. The dollar you gave in perks is in effect worth about $1.20 to you, because of the extras you do not have to pay.

One possible perk: let your accountant do employee tax returns. If he can get them a bigger refund than they would have gotten doing it themselves, you have put money in their pockets. It's as good as a raise and it's a lot cheaper if you can pay your accountant $25 and get them a $300 refund. And it is perfectly legitimate. It's a sorry commentary on our society that a perk beats money, but that's the way it is.

The law on perquisites changes virtually every year, and at the present time almost all of them have to be reported as income. Your accountant ought to keep up with the tax law and advise you of changes. If the perks do have to be reported, your accountant may be able to help you wash them out with fancy bookkeeping.

Subterfuges

Some employers take on workers and try to pass them off as self-employed independent contractors so that the employer can get out of paying social security and unemployment. I don't advise this, unless there is some real basis to the claim. The IRS is taking an active interest in this subterfuge, and justly so.

The major test is this: are they out of your care and custody? If somebody is writing your advertising copy, and she's working on her own time, and not working by the hour but by the project, and you don't know at any given time whether she is actually working, then she is actually an independent contractor and not an employee.

Clearly it's advantageous in some ways to claim someone is self-employed: you don't have to pay unemployment, and workman's compensation, and withholding taxes, and all that sort of thing. But it isn't a good policy to try to get around the law in this way. Suppose the person you claim to be self-employed is badly injured while on the job, and the judge decides that your designation of "independent contractor" was a subterfuge. He may impose penalties for your failure to cover the worker. In some states, the award is automatically tripled. And because there was no coverage, it all comes out of your own pocket.

Sometimes people will ask you to be paid "off the books." My reply would be that I don't know how I'm going to get along without you, but I'll have to try. If you pay people off the books, where do you get the money from, and how do you account for its expenditure? This money has to show up somewhere—or else you have to hide it, and that's illegal.

Of course it's well known that there's an enormous underground economy in operation in this country making unreported money; but if you're just starting out in business and have so much else to worry about, should you get involved in all these illegal maneuvers? And even if you are able to get away with it while you have a tiny operation, you can't possibly do it when you get bigger, when you're no longer a one-person business working out of a pay telephone. When you grow to any size you'll have to have somebody else handling your money, and now you've got to trust that person to cover your tracks.

If your off-the-books employee is injured, he will probably bring action against you, causing great embarrassment and penalties. A lot of difficulties arise from accommodating people who want to be paid "off the books," and I don't want to sound oppressively moral, but I'd steer clear of it.

Temporary and Part-time Employees

They are expensive but sometimes worth it. A lot of the expense comes from the agency taking its cut. But it certainly makes sense if you only need a few people for a few days—unloading a trailer, for example. You pay an average of $9 an hour, about twice your usual rate. If you need a typist for a week or so who can hit fifty words per minute, you'll pay a premium, but you don't have to do the screening, interview six people to find the right one, and the like.

Part-time workers frequently work out well. They're often young women who are also wives and mothers and who are eager to work but can't do it full-time. And you just may not be able to afford to keep people employed full-time. Even in offices where full-time employment is the rule, a lot of job-sharing is going on, often with two women sharing a job. They're happy because it suits their needs; and you can probably pay them less than you would one full-time employee. They will accept a little less because they are being accommodated.

Tipping Situations

Waiters and waitresses have a special minimum wage below the amount set for other workers: official government recognition of the fact that much of their income comes via tipping. But if the employee does not make a total amounting to the minimum wage the employer has to make up the difference. If the restaurant has more than eight employees, the employer has to keep track of the volume of each waiter and waitress. If he or she does $500 in volume, $40 has to be declared in tips. This amounts to a lot of extra record-keeping for the owner, although the new sophisticated cash registers are undoubtedly able to provide all this data.

A Very Mild Horror Story

Only once did an employee do me in. Our summer camp classified counselors in two categories: team and senior. The team counselors were younger, usually sixteen years old, and functioned as a team of two for each group of youngsters they counseled. The senior counselors were older, eighteen to twenty years, functioned alone, and were paid more. On the first day of camp one summer, a young woman showed up whom I had interviewed but had not hired. I told her that I had not offered her a job. She said I had. I did not agree but I said Okay, I still have one opening and you can have it, but it's for a team counselor. She said she would love to have it.

By the middle of summer she had quit, but I eventually heard from her again. She complained to the state labor department that she was over eighteen years of age and should have been paid the higher rate and wanted the back pay supposedly due her. She won the case and cost me a lot of money and time defending myself as well; and the state labor department lived in my office for the better part of a month, combing through my records. It was an unhappy experience all around.

Having a Replacement

This was brought to my attention in a rather vivid fashion when I crashed my airplane. Although I had delegated most of my business to employees, I was holding on to certain areas as my turf—making bank deposits and payroll, among others.

All of a sudden I was out of the picture. I hadn't really prepared anyone to do any of these things. That was a major mistake. Not that I shouldn't have done it myself, but I should have had a surrogate who had some notion of what I was doing in these areas, who could step in at such a crisis as this. Except for my accountant, nobody knew exactly what each of my employees was getting paid, especially with regard to extra perks, management fees, and the like.

Fortunately my wife, a couple of employees, and some of the older children jumped in and took over. But I decided that I would not let this happen again.

Now I have a master list that ticks off what I do and how I do it.

Take the crisis scenario into account. If something happens, if you have cardiac arrest or are otherwise put totally out of commission, there should be some kind of game plan that everybody understands, so that the others can pick up the slack as well as possible. If you don't do that, eight weeks in the hospital can wipe out your business. If you have a game plan, there's a chance you'll still have a business when you come back.

In my case the business was mature enough to withstand my absence. I was lucky because there were other times in my career when I'm not sure my business could have taken the shock and survived.

Cutting the Grass

We live in an age of increasing specialization. I'm not always happy with the effects of this tendency, but it's unmistakable. Even retailing has swung back to specialty stores. Less and less often do you find somebody who does it all. Even in a small operation, it's often the case that the financial person, the marketer, and the manufacturer are different people performing different specialties. I'd like to show you yet another reason why you should welcome help.

Let's say your grass needs cutting. To save the cost of hiring a neighborhood child, you do it yourself. The moment you get behind, or astride, that lawnmower, you are working for the minimum wage. That's what you could get it done for. As the executive head of your business, can you afford to work for such money?

If you enjoy cutting grass or regard it as good exercise, fine then, do it. But don't delude yourself into thinking that it's a savings. You're engaged in a form of recreation that is costing you money. Most guys don't like to cut grass. If all your time is worth is the minimum wage, close up your business and get a job because you can do a lot better than that in the job market.

Cutting the grass yourself is a false kind of economizing. You can use your abilities for something more productive. You could be sitting at your desk thinking of ways to increase sales; or out looking for new products; or relaxing, so that when you get back to your desk you will be more productive. If you really enjoy posting the books—although I find that hard to believe—then do it late at night when the day's thinking is over; otherwise, get someone else to do it.

Since my flower shop is situated across the street from my house, I used to be in it all the time. Intellectually I knew that it didn't pay for me to be over there waiting on customers, but emotionally I couldn't let it go. The plane crash of 1982 that almost killed me changed my mind. For months I never stepped inside the door of the shop, and it went on functioning as well as ever and made more money than it had when I was popping in every day.

A friend of mine named Al runs a contracting company. Once when I went to see him in his office I looked down into the yard to behold a shambles—trucks broken down and employees running like ants in all directions in an enactment of Murphy's Law.

Al was sitting at his desk with his feet up, chatting with me, and he asked me if I'd like to play cards. I suggested that he might be needed downstairs, that it looked as if the moment of maximum crisis had arrived.

"The day I've got to go down there and straighten the situation out," he said, "I'm a failure. I'm supposed to be up here thinking. I'm creating jobs. I can hire people to go out and fix what's wrong down there."

He was right. If you have the capacity to create, that's what you should be doing. You should be doing what you do best, not what you can hire someone else to do. But there may be times in your business when you literally cannot afford to take that position, and you may have to do the donkeywork yourself. That's the price you pay for poverty—you do minimum-wage work. But on balance it doesn't pay.

All people are created unequal, but they are given an equal amount of time in the day. If it takes you an hour to do what an accountant can do in ten minutes, and your time is better spent selling your product, hire the accountant. It's cheaper.

The Importance of Employees

Here are a couple of stories that illustrate what difference an employee makes.

Story one: I travel first class. One reason is that I like the comfort. I carry on clothes, and I like them gently hung up in a closet because when I get off the plane my day is frenetically programmed, with every minute accounted for. I don't have time to spend three hours calling valet service in the hotel to have my suit or tuxedo pressed.

When I got on the plane on this occasion, I was the only first-class passenger, but the closet was full. I told the stewardess (or, to keep up with the times, the flight attendant) that I would like to hang up my clothes. She said she was sorry, but the closet was full and I should put them in the overhead.

"Whose luggage is this?" I asked. Then I answered my own question. "It's the crew's luggage." I sent for the captain.

When he came out and introduced himself, I asked him: "Why do you suppose I'm paying $725 to ride in the same plane the guy in the back is paying $180 to ride in? I want a wide seat, maybe a glass of juice while we're still on the ground. Most important, I want to hang up my clothes."

"You're absolutely right," he said. He called the stewardess over and told her to move her clothes out. She was unhappy about it. She was, by the way, head stewardess.

I always vote with my feet. On the way back, I changed my tickets and rode with another airline. The first one lost my fare, which isn't going to help their considerable financial difficulties. If enough employees burn off enough customers, there won't be any more airline. That same airline spends astronomical sums every year on TV advertising but doesn't know what its employees are doing. And make no mistake, it's the employer's responsibility to see that it doesn't happen.

Story two shows how just the opposite happened in a small hotel chain in Baton Rouge. One of the extras that this chain offers is a complimentary breakfast. I was beat, going on very little sleep, and had an early plane to catch. I walked out of my room with my bag (the bellhops all being asleep at 5:15 A.M.), and from eight stories below, wafting up the atrium, came the smell of frying bacon.

On the main floor I saw a middle-aged black woman cooking in the little restaurant. I asked her what time it opened.

"Six thirty," she said.

"At that time," I said, "I expect to be about forty thousand feet in the air."

"Well," she asked, "can I make you something now?"

That restaurant was not opening for another hour. She was not getting paid to open for me. Nevertheless she made me some toast and bacon, which was all I wanted, and made a most favorable impression on me for the hotel chain in which she filled a rather modest position. I'll go back to that chain again, because one of their employees cared about me.

Employees Know Things That You Don't

A young lady had just begun her career as a trainee at a small branch of a major bank. Part of her training consisted of reviewing account applications that had been denied to learn the reasons for denials, and among them she came across one that interested her.

It was an application of a young man who was denied because he had no banking history. He had asked to have his paychecks mailed to the bank because he traveled, and he was quite young.

The trainee picked up the telephone and called the number on the card. She said if he would come in she would personally see to it that he got a checking account. The young man was surprised because the woman he had talked to earlier had rejected his application. The young lady assured him that she would work something out for him. He came in and was quite grateful for the consideration.

The reason the young lady recognized the name was that he was a rock star who had just packed Madison Square Garden. He had a seven-figure annual salary and was willing to put it in an interest-free checking account, which would make a lot of money for the bank. But the thirty-five-year-old woman manager had never heard of him. To her he was just a long-haired kid in jeans.

There are a lot of lessons in this. Don't kick away a lot of business on a superficial assessment. Ask a few more questions. And give your employees time to make good evaluations. Frequently they are being required to grind through so many applications per week that they don't have the time to do anything beyond the superficial. In this case the bank made out all right because of an alert young trainee.

What I'm trying to convey to you is that these are management errors, not employee errors. You can't blame the clerks—it's the people who make the policy who take the bows for successes and should take the black eyes for failure.

Family

The basic product you expect from your family is unqualified support. Running your enterprise—with competitors undercutting your prices, the federal bureaucracy inventing new forms to fill out, the local government measuring the width of your parking spaces, your suppliers letting you down on deadlines, your customers demanding preferential treatment—is difficult enough without waffling at home.

One of the classic problems of would-be entrepreneurs who call me is that they can't come up with any capital because their wives will not stand for mortgaging the house. (It happens this way most of the time, although sometimes it's the other way around—a husband blocking a wife from a business venture.) When that's the situation, he can kiss that million-dollar surefire idea of his good-bye.

Some wives cannot get over the disappearance of the weekly paycheck. I have a friend who lost a high-paying job with a major corporation after many years in its service. He had always been good with his hands and so, instead of looking for another corporate job, he went into the woodworking business. After a difficult start, he eventually made out well and is still doing it. But his wife was tugging at him all the way. She wanted that check. Ernie, she used to say, knock off this crazy stuff and get *a real job!*

Other families have the step-down problem. Going into business for yourself means an initial lowering of expenses and thus a change in lifestyle. Some spouses accept that in good grace, others nag about it to the point of separation.

If you cannot get total support from your family, especially from your spouse, you really should not go into business for yourself. A business is a demanding mistress. It's especially so at the beginning. It won't be unusual for you to be working Saturdays and Sundays. It may mean not getting home for dinner, or missing the big Blue and Gold scout affair.

You may be getting ready to leave for the day when your best customer calls; he says he knows it's short notice, but he has to have 2,000 Type C widgets by the next morning, or else he'll try somewhere else. You, the boss, are going to roll up your sleeves and run the machines. And this was the night you had tickets to the show that you bought six months in advance, with reservations for a late dinner at a great restaurant with your best friends. But you will not be able to go. Your oldest son will fill in for you, or your wife will go with your friends, or you will try to get away in time to make the dinner. If you have been in business for yourself, you have been in that position so often that you have learned to live with it. Almost everybody in business has had to face that choice—it really is not a choice at all—and knows the pressure it puts on the marriage and the family.

If you feel a compulsion to go into business for yourself and your spouse feels equally compelled to oppose it, chances are you are going to lose either your dream or your spouse. You have to make a choice. The strain of opposing goals wears hard on a marriage, and doesn't help the business much either. The effort to survive is probably pressure enough.

When you face this kind of a basic impasse, you have to sit down with your spouse and reach a decision. Everything should be examined openly, but there can be no compromises or negotiating. One side has to prevail. Getting a three-year trial period from your spouse to make it in business is unacceptable. You'll have enough pressures without listening to the meter running at home.

If the choice is between your business or your spouse, that's a choice you'll have to make yourself.

The other extreme—a man and wife working together as partners in an enterprise—is something I don't recommend. It's an overdose of togetherness. Some people have a tolerance for it and a few even thrive on it. But what will you and your spouse talk about in your off hours? You already know everything that's happening to each other. That strains a marriage too.

Working with your sons and daughters, on the other hand, should be a joy. Our children all worked as counselors at our summer camp—and they called me "Mister" while on the job (so as to be less conspicuous). I gave them all the worst jobs, to show that I didn't favor them, but we all enjoyed it.

Three of my children, all adults, are working with me now in various enterprises. Note that I said with me, not for me; each has an equity interest in the enterprise that they are operating. The most important thing is that they have a choice, that they are not intimidated into working with their father.

9

Coping with a Complex Society

Not long ago a woman called me up with enthusiastic plans for a business. Everybody who tries her cake, she said, calls it the best ever. They had been urging her to market it commercially, so she baked several cakes, made the rounds of a few local stores, and let the owners try a sample. The storeowners were greatly impressed with her cake and offered to sell them. Now, she asked me happily, what do I do next?

First, I advised her, you cannot bake your cakes at home. Astonished at this, she asked why not. I explained that the Board of Health would not allow her to mingle her cake ingredients in the same refrigerator and pantry that the family uses, or bake her cake in a stove used for family cooking.

Furthermore, I added, chances are that your house is not in the right zone to operate that kind of a business, so you'll have to appear before a town board to get a variance to do it. Perhaps, in fact, you'll be turned down.

Thirdly, you will have to get yourself a good insurance policy that protects you against product liability. Even if the Board of Health lets you operate the business out of your home, and even if the town gives you a variance, you will never be able to find an insurance company willing to underwrite coverage for a cake product that you bake in a communal stove. It's just too difficult to defend in court.

Fourthly, you will have to establish a corporation for your business. If you are making a product that people eat, odds are that you will be sued eventually. Somebody will say that eating your cake produced hearing loss and will want to take everything you've earned in your business as well as your house and car. You need the corporate shield.

The woman who had called with such sprightliness just a few minutes earlier was mentally reeling by the time she got off the telephone. I certainly had not made her day brighter. But that's the way things are now. The delicious fudge that Aunt Minerva first made for her family and friends and then began to sell throughout the state and eventually became nationally famous —that's a story that if it happens today is a darn sight more complicated than it was in Grandma's day.

There were a number of things I had forgotten to tell my caller. I forgot to mention, for instance, that if you intend to sell cakes, you have to weigh them and mark the weight on the package, even if you don't sell them by weight. You have to use a scale that has been approved and inspected by a governmental weights and measures department—in most states, a function of the county government. There may be other packaging and labeling laws in various localities, such as listing all the ingredients. If you are going to sell the cake in Pennsylvania you need a license from the Pennsylvania Department of Agriculture.

That's all part of the complicated scene in which we live. It can be frustrating. There are some good historical reasons why food is regulated: adulterated or spoiled food was sold in the past that made people ill or killed them, and so on. The price we pay for the mistakes of the past is a complicated and often business-inhibiting system.

A Simpler Time

My first employment included the task of putting pieces of meat into a grinder to make hamburger. I was twelve years old.

The man who hired me for the job was not an exploiter of youth; he just thought I was equal to the task. Can you imagine what would happen today if he hired a twelve-year-old kid to run a meat grinder, and the youngster suffered some mishap?

Sometimes I yearn for that old simplicity. Life has become so complicated today: certainly business enterprise has. When I went into business a quarter-century ago, I didn't even carry liability insurance on my car. That couldn't be done today. I had no product liability coverage, but I certainly wouldn't take that chance today. The new, regulated society can be found in the law courts, in the federal bureaucracies, and in the state licensing boards. Where it strikes the small businessman most immediately, however, is in local government.

Government produces a good proportion of our troubles. Given that condition, it ought to provide a solution to at least half of the troubles it creates. The care and feeding of politicians is important. In any enterprise you are in a position to do favors for people. Do them.

Local Government

A fellow in Cleveland asked my opinion of his plans to buy some property in Florida. "I think it's a big mistake," I said.

"Why?" he asked.

"Buy property in Cleveland," I said. "This is where you have influence. If you have a problem with the building inspector, you can call somebody and discuss it, because you *are* somebody. In Tampa, you're just another damned carpetbagger, and don't go giving our boys a hard time."

On your own turf, when something happens against your interests, you know somebody. Now, I'm not talking about putting in the fix. I'm just saying that such difficulties can be smoothed over, especially if a friend of yours knows the public official who is causing you problems.

That's the way local government works. Most books about

business give the subject short shrift. But I've been on both sides of the fence, as a local businessman and a local official, and I know how important it is. You can argue about whether local government and its regulations cause more good or more harm, but one fact is indisputable—it adds to the cost of doing business.

Police

The police impinge on the operation of your business in countless ways. They are worth having as friends. Give the cop a 20 or 25 percent discount. It costs you a little profit, but it's a good investment. When you call the police to report a burglary or someone who is hassling one of your customers, you want to be sure that the police know you as a good guy. Not that they wouldn't do their duty for any citizen. But let's face it, they eat in your diner all the time at bargain prices. That bit of Machiavellian advice may infuriate some solid citizens, but that's the way the real world works.

And when the police come around with tickets to benefit the Patrolman's Benevolent Association, buy tickets. They need money, and they will remember, have no fear about that. Now you can complain that it's wrong, that Justice should be blindfolded. That blindfold was taken off a long time ago.

When a customer pulls up in front of your place and runs inside, he may not have noticed the yellow no-parking line painted along the curb. If he's only in there a minute or so, the police don't have to be overly zealous in slapping parking tickets on the car. It's up to them. I don't mean they ought to let him park there for an hour. But they can be a little tolerant for a minute or so—or they can be especially hard-nosed if they don't like you. You will also have deliveries coming in, and it's probably impossible to make the delivery without committing some minor infraction of traffic laws. Or you may have a group of troublesome kids hanging around outside your store—not a high-priority item for a busy police force, but if you buy the tickets and give the discounts, it might be a number two priority instead of a number fifteen. I don't view these realities as corruption but as the way things are.

Zoning

The most inescapable problem for a small businessman is zoning. Houston is the only major city in the United States free of it. Yet although zoning has spread like a sticky syrup all over America, it is a relatively new concept that has only come along since World War II.

Zoning contributes markedly to property values. A suburban one-acre lot if zoned for a one-family home might be worth $10,000. If zoned for four one-family homes, the same lot might be worth $30,000. If zoned for high-rise apartments, it could be worth $1 million. Nor can you afford to impose a lower-priced use on land zoned for a more lucrative and consequently more intensive use.

Under zoning, certain uses of land are permitted and others prohibited in various sections of a municipality. The Planning Board develops and amends the Master Plan, which allots land use for commercial, industrial, or residential purposes.

Although the Planning Board does most of the work, the governing body of the municipality usually has the final say in adopting the Master Plan.

Under such a Plan, a great number of lots and land uses will fail to conform to local requirements. In most municipalities a Zoning Board of Adjustment is set up to which people may apply for relief if this be the case. The Zoning Board grants permission to use the land despite the owner's failure to conform to the zoning ordinance. (In some cases it makes recommendations to the governing body on whether to grant such permission.)

Cases come to the Zoning Board of Adjustment for two reasons.

The first reason: the land involved is deficient in some respect. For example, a 200-foot frontage is required and the lot in question has only 180 feet of frontage. The board is asked to grant a variance because there is no reasonable way to come up with another 20 feet of frontage.

The second reason for appearing before a Zoning Board is to permit a "non-conforming use" of the land, such as a business use in a residential zone. The petitioner must show why such a use should be allowed.

You ought to have a variance even for a little home-based business. You may think that you don't want to attract attention to your business by applying for one, since you regard it as an unobtrusive little pursuit that no one notices or cares about. So you give a few piano lessons to some specially selected young students. You're not hurting anybody. What happens, however, if your dog messes on your neighbor's lawn and he takes a sudden dislike to you and turns you in? Now you have a problem because you have been operating illegally in violation of the ordinance.

In the town in which I served as mayor, an illegal building operated for several years. Set far back off the road and thus not highly visible, it was nevertheless a large building erected without a permit, and went unchallenged for a long time. It was not until the town underwent a tax revaluation that the municipal officials discovered that a lot carried on the tax books as a vacant tract was actually being used by an automobile towing company. The company then had to go to the Zoning Board of Adjustment to get a variance to put up a building that was already constructed—and if the variance had not been granted the building would have been ordered demolished. The town granted the variance but held tough bargaining sessions to set up payment of a number of years of back taxes due on the property.

Realities of Local Politics

The first thing you should do when starting a business is to buy a copy of the town's zoning ordinance and read it carefully. Don't take the word of the present landowner or of the real estate salesperson trying to sell you the lot. I'm not suggesting that they would misrepresent the facts, but that they may interpret the zoning ordinance differently than the way it is interpreted in Town Hall, or it may have been recently amended. Read it yourself. It isn't that hard to read and doesn't take a superbrain. It does take some time, however, and some attention, because it is cross-referenced like crazy. If after reading it you are still not sure that you understand it, have an attorney knowledgeable in zoning read and interpret it for you. It may be the least expensive attorney's fee you'll ever pay, and save you oceans of grief.

People commonly think that if an area is zoned for "business," your business can move right in without any obstacles. But a business zone can exclude certain business uses; a light industrial zone can exclude various industries; a residential zone may ban apartments or homes of a certain size.

For example, let's say you want to open a beauty shop. The area is zoned for "neighborhood business," and the plan lists a dozen permitted neighborhood businesses—pizza shop, delicatessen, and so on. It does not, however, mention a beauty shop as a permitted use. Neither does it exclude such a use. Is a beauty shop a neighborhood business? Or is it by its nature a regional business, drawing people from a radius well outside the neighborhood? In most cases the city would probably find in your favor—that although the beauty shop was omitted from the list it was not thereby excluded. The decision, however, could go the other way. If it does you can still go to the zoning board and seek a variance.

Or you may find yourself before a town board even on a permitted use. Just because the zoning ordinance specifically allows restaurants in the zone, for example, does not mean that

155

your fast-food operation will get a brass-band welcome. It's seldom that smooth. There are reasons why your particular proposal may be unacceptable. And if the neighborhood residents oppose your proposal—in some areas cholera is more popular than fast-food businesses—you may be in for a roller coaster ride.

The town may play along with the local residents. If they don't want you, their principal weapon is time. They will keep you coming back month after month. They will find any excuse to postpone the hearing. Their sessions will last interminably. The public will nitpick you to despair. Maybe you will be able to wait it out. If it's one of a dozen units you may be able to afford such delays, but if this is your only means of livelihood, they will probably be able to wear you down until you wave the white flag.

Towns differ in how they expedite matters. In some you'll get a quick decision. In others you will be led around by the nose for months. You'll hire lawyers, sit through record-breaking marathon sessions, and then end up with a rejection. But communities in which things like this happen develop a reputation for it—and you ought to ask about it through the businesspeople in the town.

If you have to appear before the Planning Board or the Zoning Board it often pays to have a lawyer. In some states if you are doing business as a corporation you must be represented by an attorney. If you are not articulate before a group, your lawyer will mount a more effective presentation of your case than you will. Even if you want to appear for yourself, it helps to have a lawyer in the background to aid in the folderol that accompanies such applications. For instance, the request for a variance has to be advertised at your expense in a specifically named newspaper. In most jurisdictions you must notify everyone within 200 feet of the property of your application for a variance, and to do that, the municipal lot record must be checked. The proper procedure for notifying these property owners must be followed. If you miss, or improperly notify, even a single property owner, your variance may be rescinded even after it has been granted. So a lawyer can be helpful. It pays to have a lawyer rooted in the community, because juice counts. If he can walk into Town Hall and wave hello to the mayor, it couldn't hurt.

A cautionary note: there is no uniformity whatever in zoning. An "R-2 Zone" in one town may bear only slight resemblance to the same designation in the next town; the letter prefix suggests that both are some variety of residential zone, but that's all you can assume. One "R-2 Zone" may allow garden apartments but not high-rise apartments; another may allow only single-family dwellings on a certain prescribed lot size. If you are doing business in five different towns you ought to be familiar with five different zoning ordinances.

Local Authority

Only by examples is it possible to suggest the literally countless ways that local government impinges upon your business. Let's just look at the strictures a municipality will impose on your little painted shingle—the one you hang out to notify the public of the nature of your business. What are you permitted to do with signs? What are you prohibited from doing? Are you allowed to have a flashing sign? Is a lighted sign allowed? Lighted from the outside, or must it be interior lighting, like an incandescent bulb? How large may it be? Any prohibition on colors? Placement? Height? Width? Wording? A local ordinance undoubtedly takes great pains to answer these questions.

A sign seems like a minor consideration, but it isn't. It may be the factor that makes your business a success. Take one of those 100-foot service station signs. If your station is located at the exit of an interstate highway, you want one of those signs that says "24 hours" on it, because most of your trade is coming off that exit. And if the town won't let you erect it, how is anybody winging down that highway going to know that you're there?

Owning a restaurant would bring you in repeated contact with the town's health department. They may tell you whether or not you may use automatic dishwashers, what water temperature is required for cleaning pots and dishes, what kind of health courses are required of your employees, and whether they must take the course before they begin employment.

Local officials, fortified with ordinances, will be able to dictate a surprisingly wide range of your activities. They may be able to require certain kinds of visual screening from the road. They may be able to set parking requirements, including places for handicapped drivers. They may also have final say over the following:

- How high your building may be
- What color its exterior may be
- How many urinals you must have in your men's room
- Where you will be allowed to park your vans.

If you are planning to start a restaurant in a building that formerly housed a hardware business, you may find that the appointments include only a single washroom, while the city fathers, for a restaurant of your size, require men's and women's rooms of a spaciousness to rival the Radio City Music Hall.

When you take over an existing activity, a new certificate of occupancy may be required. That's common procedure. If the business has been there a long time under the same owner, it has probably not been inspected in many years, and all kinds of violations may lie buried within. The wiring may be dangerously overloaded, for one thing, and other legitimate safety interests may be involved. In a reasonable community such a situation can be worked out. Since you can be sure that a blind inspector could find enough violations to put you out of business, the inspection may create problems for you if the officials go beyond legitimate safety concerns and into the game of "finding violations." Someone may have put in a sewer trap in 1937 and never got a permit—that sort of thing.

Before you buy a building you should be aware of the upgrading statutes in the community. In some communities, if you make any renovation whatsoever you will have to bring the whole building up to the standards of the new zoning code. If you do not make the renovations, however, the building might well be exempt from the new zoning code if it was constructed before the code was adopted. Just moving a sink or putting in a new partition may be regarded as "renovation." That might mean, as a horrible example, that you would be required to "restack" (build new vent stacks) for the entire building. That could run into big money and make the project unfeasible.

Reasonableness is what you should seek in a town government. If you have no choice about where you are going to locate your business, because despite its drawbacks it's the only place to be, that's something you have to live with. If the town requires that every building has a colonial motif to its design, that's the way you'll have to design it. But if you are able to choose where your business goes, you may be interested in testing one town against another as possible locations. A town with a positive business climate may be important to the success of your enterprise.

That reasonableness may be critical to you someday. When my son and I got out of the rental car business we were sitting with enough cars on our hands to fill a stadium.

While we were running the business, they were never a storage problem because most of them were out in the hands of customers. Like a juggler keeping most of the balls in the air, we kept most of the cars out of the garage.

But once we were out of business we were the owners of an ocean of cars. We made a deal with a neighbor to park them in his field, but he was ticketed for having too many unlicensed cars on his property, a violation of a town ordinance. Actually the cars were not unlicensed—we had taken the plates off so they wouldn't be stolen—but we didn't take issue with that because we knew the town could find some other ordinance we were transgressing.

I called the landowner and asked for three weeks. He agreed. Then I called the municipal manager and asked for the same. Well, he knew that it would take three weeks to bring the case to court anyway. So he was not losing anything, and he had a chance to do me a favor. I had been mayor and knew most of the people in local affairs. So he agreed. As it turned out, we disposed of the whole fleet in a week. But I had that grace period mostly because I had been able to help others in the past.

I've always made it my business to know the local politicians wherever I have been in business, and to make a contribution to the right party. Which party is that, you ask? That's both parties.

Politicians need money to run campaigns. Posters and mailings and advertising and poll watchers all take money. They have to get this money from someone, and they remember where it came from. Anybody in business who doesn't make contributions—I'm not talking about big numbers, just $100 or $200—is foolish. It's worth it. If you think that's horrible, you'll have to change a system that's been impregnable for a long time.

Licensing

If you are able to shop around for a town in which to locate, ask what kind of a licensing policy is in effect. Some towns stress quick action, while others tend to become mired in rigmarole. If you have begun to pay rent, purchased space in the Yellow Pages, and then cannot open for a few months because of a town's complicated licensing procedures, it could wound your business mortally. Some towns will not issue a license in advance; you must be the current tenant before any official action can begin. That can cause snarls.

Be sure to check with the town if your business needs to be licensed. There are basically three varieties of governmental licenses: professional licenses (for doctors, lawyers, and teachers, for example) to protect the public from incompetent people; licenses issued for dangerous or socially controlled substances, such as junkyards, pollution equipment, plumbing, liquor, or cigarettes; and revenue licenses, which are issued (theoretically at least) to cover the expenses created by your business—the cost of health inspections, paperwork, and the like. Licensing fees should not be designed as a revenue-producer for the town. Some towns, however, use them for that purpose, charging inordinately high fees. One town, on one side of the road, may charge $500 for a license that costs $10 in another town on the other side of the road. Such a fee is not going to plunge your business into insolvency. But you ought to be aware of these differences and, all else being equal, you might consider the location with the more reasonable fee—especially since the fee might indicate fundamental attitudes toward business.

Payoffs

Sometimes all that you pay for a license (or for zoning approval) is not shown on the official town fee list. Sometimes an unofficial price list is also in effect. It's not impossible to learn by reputation whether a town is run honestly or not, and you may want to avoid a town with a history of corrupt practices.

You may otherwise find yourself with a permanent, though probably minor, drain on your resources. Or, all of the corruption may be up front, when approval time comes. You might be asked to buy a lot of overpriced tickets to a dance, and then find that approval of your license will be forthcoming.

Never, never make overtures to a public official. You may find your assumption about his intentions wrong and find yourself in a lot of trouble. If the official is interested in a payoff, he will make it unmistakably clear to you. I leave the moral decision in your hands. The legal implications should be obvious to you.

Although corruption in public life is by no means rare, most politicians—contrary to the prevailing folklore—are not dishonest. My experience in politics has shown me that stupidity is a much more endemic problem than corruption. And in some ways for business, stupidity is worse.

Had I a choice to make between a dumb official and a corrupt one, I would probably for the sake of my business choose the dishonest one. Corruption is annoying, but stupid politicians can drive you into bankruptcy. In purely practical terms, I prefer the payoff to the long and grueling hearings, the high legal fees, in pursuit of an approval that never comes because the politicians are too stupid to have a good business climate in the town.

The Case Against Child Safety

Beyond local government with its strictures lie the mammoth institutions of state and federal government. In addition to fulfilling all the rules of local officials, many businesses also require a state license—day care centers and nursery schools, to name two examples.

Beyond that, how much the state and federal government pester you depends on the business you're in. Small operations generally are not the target of the government's affirmative action programs. (I've always had enough women and minorities working for me that it would not be a problem if they came around anyway.) One of the compensations of running a tiny business is that the bureaucratic nitpickers don't bother you as much. There're too many tiny businesses for them.

Nothing can be more irritating than the self-righteous bureaucrat armed with his book of regulations. The unreasonableness of bureaucrats administering the state child safety laws helped to drive me out of the nursery school and camp business a few years ago.

How can anybody be against child safety? Yet a group of state inspectors found me to be the sort of person who lets children drown in wading pools. They came in, unsmiling and forceful, to see my summer camp operation. Some years earlier I had built a number of outdoor fireplaces scattered about the area so that the kids could cook their own hot dogs and hamburgers. The inspectors informed me that the fireplaces were unsafe and had to be moved.

"Why?" I asked.

"Because you're going to set these trees on fire," they said.

I had the fireplaces set under trees so that youngsters wouldn't broil in the sun while they were cooking. "Those fireplaces have been there for ten years and have never scorched a single leaf," I said. "I'll tell you what. I'll give you a gallon of gasoline and a book of matches, and if you can burn a leaf on that tree I'll move the fireplaces."

And they said: "You'll move them, or we'll close you down."

One of the child safety requirements was the Lost Swimmer Drill. Every ten minutes you have to clear the area of swimmers and have lifeguards swim along shoulder to shoulder looking for bodies. I had at that time three pools. The officials were willing to grant that there was no need to perform the drill in the wading pool, which was only a few inches deep, but that it had to be done as per regulations in the other two pools.

"My eyesight isn't that great," I said, "but I'll tell you what. I'll take a coin out of my pocket and throw it into the pool. If it lands heads I'll read you the date."

As they stood there, I quickly did it. Then I suggested that the regulation they were talking about was designed, and reasonably so, for ponds, lakes, and rivers and that it wasn't really necessary to send teams of frogmen swimming through my little pools looking for bodies.

They said: "Every ten minutes, or your operation is shut down."

They had a persuasive way about them. So, fed up, I sold the nursery school and camp that year. I was afraid harm would

163

come to these officials by my own hands. They were young men just out of college, sure that the only way to keep the world orderly and safe was to hog-tie everybody with rules.

I escaped some of the later insanities. My successor had to post guards at every window, because otherwise a child might fall through the window and be cut. They could have insisted, to be safer, that the glass be replaced with some unbreakable plastic. They also insisted that the buses taking the kids to and from camp have matrons in attendance. The same kids who rode to school ten months of the year without a matron had to have one in the summer when they rode the same bus, with the same driver, to camp.

Unfortunately, all this wonderful governmental protection is not free. The last van that I bought before leaving the camp business cost $20,000 because of all the required safety features. It all costs, and the parents have to pay for it because it's written into the costs of camp. It's no wonder that camp is beyond the means of many families today.

Deep Pockets

The other major change that has complicated business is product liability. It has been running roughshod over big business. One airplane company stopped making four highly popular small planes. The reason? Because 37 percent of the cost of the airplane was insurance payments—against possible future accidents. At the present writing, I believe, there is only one IUD manufacturer in the country—not because the product is considered unsafe, but because the companies can't afford to pay the premium.

Not long ago a jury ruled against a motor boat manufacturer for product liability. One of the engines had blown up and the boat had swerved off course, seriously injuring bystanders. It had been racing through the water at great speed, and with good reason, for it was being pursued by a Coast Guard cutter. During the investigation of the accident several items came to light. 1) The boat was fourteen years old. 2) It had been serviced by nine boatyards, none of them affiliated with the manufacturer, over that period. 3) It was being operated at speeds far in excess of manufacturer's recommendations. 4) The operators were accused of using it for illegal purposes, to wit, smuggling drugs. Unfortunately, innocent people were severely injured in the accident, but it is hard to believe that a judge and jury found a six-million-dollar award against a manufacturer who had not seen the boat in fourteen years. The cost of this award, needless to say, is now built into the price of boats.

When one of the conglomerates decided to sell off a small machine manufacturing company, it was picked up by a father and son. Unfortunately, they also picked up responsibility for a product liability suit, and the courts held them liable for damages centering on a machine manufactured ten years before the father was born. (He was in his fifties.) It's absurd but true.

If you buy a business from someone else it's best, in these crazy times, not to take over the corporation. Form another corporation with a somewhat different name, if that's possible. If you're buying Jack Rabbit Polka-Dot Ties, Inc., form a new corporation and call it Jack Rabbit Polka-Dot and Striped Ties, Inc. That may not save you from corporate liability—the courts will agonizingly decide that—but it can't hurt.

The name of the game in this litigation-crazy society is Deep Pockets—trying to find someone who will pay. Guilt doesn't matter anymore. All that matters is whether you have the money. If I'm 99 percent at fault and you're 1 percent at fault, but you have the money and I don't, it's likely that the jury will make you pay.

Liability insurance drove me out of the car-rental business. Our coverage costs just kept increasing to the point that we could no longer bear it. And what happened to us has been happening to car-rental companies all over the nation. The very big ones can afford a partial self-insurance program, and they deal in such big money that the insurance company is interested in the cash flow. But RCA sold off Hertz, for one-third of the asking price: the biggest auto rental company in the nation was sold for a little more than the price of a Los Angeles TV station.

In my estimate you should think very carefully about the product liability question before going into a business. I had a young lady call recently with an idea for a business—taking care of young children for a couple of weeks while their parents go on vacation. At one time I would have advised her to do it. But can you imagine going to an insurance man and trying to buy a policy on a business like that?

Times have changed drastically since I launched a business career, and I wouldn't be in the nursery school business today if somebody walked over and gave me the place I sold 15 years ago. I have two criteria that would govern my choice of a field to enter in these days, and they are negative criteria: first, I would favor a business with a negligible government interference factor and, second, a business with a low insurance liability factor. I wouldn't get in the drug business if I discovered a cure for cancer. I might license somebody else to it, but I wouldn't do it. No heavy insurance liability and no government in my face. It has gotten to the point where those are the primary considerations.

10

Operating Your Business

Now it's time to examine some important precepts about how to operate a business. What value, you may ask, is there in that? Can we say anything about a small business that's specific enough to be of any help? Isn't every business different? Do you mean that the little elderly lady who just opened a card shop and the big burly guy who's decided to hire out heavy equipment both have to face the same problems?

Yes, that's exactly what I mean. The similarities of what they have to face are far more important than the differences between two businesses. Those similarities begin with the general principles that must guide them and all other small businesses. Some of them have already been mentioned, but it's important enough to review them again.

Self-motivation
Whatever the business, the owner has to be self-disciplined—has to climb out of the sack when nobody is telling him to, has to work on the most gorgeous of days, has to stick with it when dinner is getting cold at home. That self-motivation is an essential quality in all business.

Attention to Details
Another point of commonality: even if you cap burning oil

wells or give skydiving displays—no matter how glamorous your business or how pedestrian—every business is filled with thousands upon thousands of details. These details are not thrilling, but they cannot be neglected. The question that you eventually have to face is: Are you going to do this work, or is somebody else going to do it?

As I have already noted, at the outset of your business you don't have any options. You have to do everything yourself. But as your business prospers and matures, you will eventually have the option of deciding that you really are not good at taking inventory and you are going to have somebody else do it. You can't do that, however, until 1) you can afford it, and 2) you understand the inventory process. If inventory is a mystery to you, you can't train an employee to do it, and furthermore, you would be at your employee's mercy, since you would not know whether it was being done effectively and honestly.

Delegating

Whatever the business, you have to learn to use people effectively. If you can't use them effectively, you can't grow. Perhaps the most difficult part of the whole operation is to stand back and let them make mistakes. Just as your children have to fall on their faces and get their noses bloodied in order to learn to walk, employees have to deal with pratfalls. Obviously there are limits, and there are times when you must hurl yourself between the employee and the catastrophe. But frequently you have to let them make mistakes and then let them extricate themselves from the mistakes. It's part of the training.

What I'm talking about is delegation. Nobody ever became successful until he learned to delegate responsibility. That includes not chastising your employee because he did it differently from the way you would have done it. This requires maturity and tolerance on your part. You're not going to keep a capable person without exhibiting those qualities because a good worker doesn't want all his decisions countermanded. It is a hard lesson to learn, especially for the entrepreneurial type who is likely to wedge himself into every decision, even down to what kind of toilet cleanser to use. That's not smart, because we only have a limited amount of time and can't be in on everything.

Being Effective

We are told that all men and women are created equal. That's horsefeathers. The fact is that we are inherently created unequal. We have been given all sorts of different skills and gifts and shortcomings in different amounts. But there is one thing we are all given equally. We all have, in each day given to us, twenty-four hours. It's how we use it that tells.

We have all met people who work sixteen hours a day. Maybe that's admirable. The fact is, however, that they probably work about five hours. Oh, they're at their desks for sixteen hours a day, all right, and they probably think they are working all that time. But they're spending a little time looking at the newspaper, and sorting out some junk mail, and doodling, and talking to a contact on the telephone. If you look closely at their day, an efficient six hours of work might have been more effective.

The most successful people that I have met use their day the most successfully. That's the key to their success. They may not always look that organized, but they are. There's a lot of truth in the old saw that if you want to get something done find a busy person to do it. A busy person will find the time.

Effective use of time is essential to operating a business. You have to find your own ways to do that, so I give you a couple of mine only by way of illustration. For one thing, I have a car telephone and return most of my calls from the car. Since I commute a hundred miles a day, I spend a lot of time in my car. There's no reason to waste it just sitting there. I also dictate in my car—or on airplanes—instead of reading or sleeping.

On airplanes I often turn down meals to keep working. This has two benefits. It keeps me from sitting there and getting fat, and it gives me work time. If I'm hungry in the morning I'll take the first meal, but sometimes in switching planes I'll be offered another meal. I keep working instead. That's important because people are flying more than ever in business.

Business has learned that it costs less to travel than to hire more people. It's cheaper for you to fly to Chicago twice a week than to open an office and staff in Chicago. More and more companies are deciding that they don't need an office in a city; they can put an executive on a plane, let him or her stay in a hotel room and do whatever needs doing. I think this trend will continue. So if you turn dead time into productive time, it's a double saving.

You'll find that you do certain tasks best at a certain time of the day, so do them at the time that's best for you. If some tasks are odious to you, it's best to do them first thing, so that they don't nag at you all day long. Get the worst part done first and the rest will seem easier.

There are many other problems and principles common to all business, and more of them will be examined later. Now that we have looked at getting started in business, the professional support you will need, and the climate in which small business thrives or withers, it's time to look at the long haul: keeping your business going, keeping records, and making the chosen business a success. But don't forget what has come earlier. Every time you remove one of the factors we've examined, you reduce your chances of success. Without having pre-examined what you're getting into, you're in trouble, unless you're really fleet on your feet. Without enough capital to support your enterprise for a reasonable period of time, you greatly increase you chances of failure. And if you take away your support system—any one of your Seven Mules—your whole enterprise can collapse.

Getting It Done

One of my first jobs as a youngster was working as a soda jerk, delivery boy, clerk, and just about everything else in Sam and Joe's Service Drug Store back in the 1940s. The proprietors consisted of one official pharmacist and one unofficial pharmacist. Joe Schaffman had graduated from the Rutgers College of Pharmacy; Sam Laifer may never have seen the inside of a high school, much less gone to college. But Sam could fill any prescription that Joe could fill, and probably knew as much about pharmacy, having learned it all on the job. This was not legal, of course, but they were well plugged in, so if the inspector from the State Pharmacy Board was heading their way, Sam went home and Joe would be standing behind the counter when he arrived.

Sam and Joe had a post office substation in the pharmacy. If you wanted a ball of twine, suntan oil, or something to patch the hole in your sneaker, they would reach under the counter and find it. The basement was filled with old tie-in goods. (During World War II, if a product was scarce a retailer would sometimes have to buy ten cases of something else to get it.) For the five years I worked there, I kept shuffling the boxes around in the basement. You couldn't give some of the stuff away, such as the sanitary napkins that were like sandpaper. We eventually sold them as polishing rags.

These guys could make do better than anyone else I've ever known. I used to patch their water pipes with adhesive tape and paint. You'd wrap the tape around the break, then dip your hands in the oil-base paint, and slop it over the tape. Then more tape, then more paint, then more tape, then more paint. When the concoction dried it worked. It didn't look good, but it worked. They were always jerry-rigging something. That was an education for me. I learned more from Sam and Joe than I ever learned at any school I ever attended.

At one point there was a severe shortage of Coca-Cola syrup.

Sam and Joe were not about to close down the soda fountain because of a little thing like that, so we concocted a pseudo-Coke syrup. I cooked it in a big pot in the back room, squatting over a gas burner that was perched on four bricks. We manufactured chocolate syrup that way on occasion, too.

They were as unalike as two partners could be. Sam was kosher; Joe had no interest in religion. Sam would never work on the Sabbath, so Joe always worked Friday nights and Saturdays.

They let me use their street corner to sell Christmas trees and mistletoe. I leaned the trees up against the outside wall. I used to think in those days that someday I'd be an owner and have kids working for me, and would want to influence them the way Sam and Joe influenced me. I suspect they influenced a lot of kids. What an education that was! I regret that neither of them lived to meet my kids.

Eventually a drug salesman who was also a pharmacist bought the store. He wanted to streamline it. When Sam and Joe had it, that was the place to be after church on Sunday—buying newspapers, getting cigarettes, drinking a Coke. The new owner threw much of that out. There's no money in selling newspapers, he decided. He took out the post office because he couldn't make any money at that. He took out most of the reasons why anyone would stop there, except for prescriptions. Six months later the place closed.

Any Which Way You Can

When you are in business for yourself you have to be a jack-of-all-trades, and sometimes you have to get things done even when people tell you it can't be done. That's what Sam and Joe taught me, and what I have had to learn over and over again.

The building in which I put my nursery school had been an old farmhouse—a big one with sixteen rooms, but certainly not more than a dozen people had lived in it. With the school we had

172

400 people using the toilets, and those septic tanks had not been designed to handle so much work. We could put in a drain field, but it would cost an enormous amount of money, and would take a lot of digging up of existing paving. I just could not afford it. On the other hand, I couldn't have water burbling out of the ground every time somebody flushed the toilet.

About two hundred yards away I had dug some gigantic holes, thirty to forty feet long and ten feet wide, with a back hoe. I had thrown debris in there that I didn't want to pay to have hauled away. Then I had lined the holes with tarpaper or canvas and had thrown rock into them.

I decided to get rid of that burbling water. We dug a trench out to those holes and installed an Orangeburg pipe—which didn't work. So we tried a one-and-a-half inch plastic pipe, which did work. Now the pits could take water forever, but it was uphill out to them, so I put a pump in the garage and another pump underground in the dry well.

I had to have a way to check the pipe, however, and glass pipe couldn't be found. So I went to the grocery store looking for something. I bought a bottle of hot sauce that looked the right size, cut the top and bottom from the bottle with a glass saw. Then I clamped the glass to the plastic pipe, so that I could look into the pipe and see what was going through.

The pump was somewhat too light for the job; I should have bought a heavy-duty industrial pump, but the expense was too much. I put a timer on it, so that every once in a while the pump would kick on, suck water out of the ground, and push it through the pipe.

What I did was illegal, and there's no way any health department in North America would ever have approved it, but had I gone the legal way I would have been bankrupted, so I did what I had to do to survive.

A big field of about ten acres that had once been farmed also lay on my school property. I needed it for a playing field. I graded and leveled it myself as best I could—plowed it, ditched it, furrowed it, and planted grass. It looked good but it was a bit uneven and rolling.

After a rainstorm, pockets of water would lie in it, three or four inches deep. Collectively that's a lot of water, and the ground wouldn't take it quickly, so after a heavy storm we couldn't use it for recreation for a week. Ultimately, the water would get into the basement; at the end of a torrential rain the basement would be dry, but a week later when the sun was shining and all the water in the field was gone, there would be a foot of it in our basement.

An engineer friend of mine looked at it and told me what had to be done. He estimated that it would cost about $10,000, which was a lot of money in the 1960s. I could not afford it.

One of my employees and I developed an idea. We found the lowest point in the field and dug a hole about six-and-a-half feet deep. We lined it with interlocking cinder block, the kind that tightens as pressure is applied to it. Then we dug trenches to the other low points and put Orangeburg pipe in the trenches. We mixed some concrete and installed a grill in the deep hole; water in the other low points would flow to this lowest point. At the bottom of the deep hole we placed a submersible sump pump. We ran a little air line out of the pump to the surface and ran an inch-and-a-half line from the deep hole out to a ditch in the road, into which the water could be pumped. Every time it rained the pump went on. Sometimes the rain would get several feet deep in that hole, but eventually the pump would catch up.

The experts will tell you how to do it right, and if you have the money, go ahead and do it the right way. If you don't have the money you have to jerry-rig something. That solution cost me about $200 and a lot of sweat.

Committee of One

When they have something that needs doing, big corporate

types call up a specialist and have it done. The small business-person can't afford that. Big corporations can have a vice president in charge of shoelace tips. The small businessman is vice president in charge of everything. That doesn't mean you try to be your own lawyer or your own accountant, but don't expect your accountant to function as an accounting department. You have to collect the facts and do a lot of the legwork. You have to be flexible and resourceful.

In the face of scarcity, you will sometimes have to make highly difficult choices. There are absolute givens such as the unalterable fact that everybody has to be paid when payday comes around. Termites, on the other hand, can wait a few days; they can't do that much more damage in another couple of days. If it's snowing and the temperature is dropping to zero, it's absolutely necessary to have antifreeze in the truck radiators. But you don't have to have snow tires on the trucks; you can keep them in the lot and deliver when the roads are safe. Sometimes, however, you *can't* wait to make the deliveries, which is why life is full of difficult choices.

Competition

It's welcome. When my son and I went looking for a location for our second rental car outlet, we looked for a place near a competitor. I'd like to be right next door to him, or right across the street. Why? Because people think of that as the area to go when they rent a car. I'll get my piece of the business because I'll be competitive.

The last place I want to be is thirty miles away from everybody else. If you were looking for a new coat, and there were four clothing stores on Main Street on the north side of town, and one clothing store on James Street on the south side, which street would you go to? I'll do more business near a competitor than I'll do away off on my own somewhere. Most major department stores will not locate in a shopping mall unless there are other department stores in the mall. They don't want to be the only game in town. When the customers come in to shop at Sears, J. C. Penney wants a shot at them as well. They want the competition there to help draw business.

To stay competitive, you have to keep on top of events. When I was in the school and summer camp business, there was a property not that far from my camp. Somebody applied to use it as a camper site, but that was rejected. As a consequence the land lay unused for a couple of years, and then a fellow came along who rented it for use as a children's day camp. One day we were in the area playing softball and I took a look at it. It was a little operation with only sixty children. My own camp had four hundred kids at the time, so I thought nothing much about it. Within two years this camp became a competitor, while I thought I was beating the world.

For years I had been upgrading my camp annually—one year I'd put in a swimming pool, the next year a golf course, and so on. Each outlay usually came to about $25,000. Then one year I decided not to plow the money back into the business. Nothing adverse happened. My business was as good as ever. So the next year I decided again to pocket the $25,000 instead of investing it in the business. Now I began to feel it; I lost one hundred kids that year. A lot of them were over in the new camp this fellow had started. He was putting his money back into the business and I wasn't.

No matter what business you are in, you have to keep looking over your shoulder when you're ahead, because sure as hell somebody is catching up on you. And when he cuts along the inside rail and passes you, it's hard to catch up with him again.

Competition can get tough. Let's say you have a pharmacy with a soda fountain and ice cream. An ice cream parlor opens next door. What are your alternatives?

First, you can decide to keep your ice cream business without a change because people come in for all sorts of things, and a certain number of them will buy a cone here rather than walk next door.

Second, you can take your ice cream business out and replace it with something unique to the shopping area. Perhaps you can reach an accommodation with the operator next door. You can concede him his ice-cream specialty, then tell him that you'd like him to stay out of the specialty candy business because you intend to open a candy counter, and the two of you will then not be competing directly (although of course you'll still be competing for the sweets dollar).

Third, if accommodation does not work, some folks would try the frontal assault. "Ice cream is only five percent of my business," one might tell the new neighbor. "Starting next week I'm selling cones at ten cents each. You certainly can't sell prescriptions. And if I keep selling cones at that price, you can't stay here long." That's the first move in a price war. Admittedly the pharmacy proprietor would lose money on ice cream but the rest of his business will help carry him. This inches into the area of unfair business practices, but don't think it doesn't happen all the time.

It may strike you as odd, but sometimes you will find yourself in competition with yourself. Here's how that sometimes happens. Suppose you have a convenience store along a well-traveled road. Two miles down the road a little neighborhood shopping center is being built. It's quite clear that the mix in that little center will include a convenience store. It may well be that it would be in your best interest for that convenience store to be yours. It's going to be there no matter what. You'll be competing with yourself, of course, but that beats competition from someone else. You have to think in such terms to survive.

That happens all the time in small business. Renting used cars has been a fairly recent development in our society, and one in which I was involved. When one of the conventional car rental operations saw a Rent-a-Wreck franchise coming into New York

City, it bought the franchise. It decided to compete, in a sense, against itself in New York. But the Rent-a-Wreck franchise was coming to New York whatever the conventional company did, and so it made the best of the situation. It's hard to hate a guy who thinks like that.

And of course big business competes against itself all the time as well. Just look in the supermarket at how many dishwashing brands or cereals belong to the same company.

Working at Home

It's distracting. Some people have a problem working at home because it's too close to the refrigerator. Children and spouses are all over the place, interfering with your work. You lose the discipline of being at the workplace at certain regular hours, which may create problems for you.

But on the positive side, all you have to do is roll out of bed and go to work. It saves a lot in commuting time and expenses, and eating at home is cheaper than restaurants.

Personally, I don't like working at home. It means you can't ever get away from the office on the one hand; on the other hand it can be isolating. (And it's too close to the refrigerator.) But for a beginning business, it saves a lot of overhead.

You can disguise the fact that you work at home, if that is an advantage to you, by taking a post office box. Sometimes you can rent a part-time office and get a mail drop with it. The arrangement sometimes includes a central telephone console that can take your phone calls and thus give the aura of a fully staffed office. I see these offers all over, so a lot of businesses must be using such cover.

My Three Rules

I have three basic rules of operation, which have stood me in good stead over the years.

1) Don't reinvent the wheel. If someone else has a good idea in sales or merchandising, use it. You can't patent or copyright an idea. If you're in the cake business, and everybody else is selling strawberry whipped cream cake, don't race out and get a corner on blueberries. If strawberries are hot, they're hot. If one of your competitors just spent a small advertising fortune promoting strawberries, take a free ride.

2) If it ain't broke, don't fix it. There's some kind of psychological need for a new person to make improvements. Why? If things are going well, keep them going well. There's no need to play genius. In my flower business it's roses. I can't improve on a rose. We keep selling them day in and week out. There's nothing else that men identify with in buying flowers as they do a rose. If you think I'm going to spend a lot of time creating a market for lilies, you don't quite understand how it works. The day that lilies start outselling roses, I'll be there selling lilies.

3) Consider the turtle; he gets no place until he sticks his neck out. You must come to realize that this does not nullify what I said earlier. But all life is full of seeming contradictions. It would be good if you could take one path and it led to riches. You have to take these contradictions, or seeming contradictions, and weave them into a tapestry.

Self-belief

I hesitate to mention this, because it sounds like inspirational material. Yet I feel compelled to say it: Unless you believe in yourself, you're not going anyplace.

When I was in college I ran a snack bar. One night a fellow I knew walked in with a paycheck for $240. In those days, $240 would have paid off the national debt. It was big money. This fellow was a really nice sort, but he had never struck me as a ball

179

of fire. Where in the world would he come up with that kind of money? Why would somebody give it to him?

He wanted me to cash his check, and I did. Afterward, I went back to the office and looked at that check for ten full minutes. It was drawn by an out-of-state company on an out-of-state bank. I called the company. I asked for the man who wrote the check.

When he came on the telephone I told him that I had this check. He assured me that the check was good. I said that I knew it was good because I already had called the bank. Well, he asked, why then are you calling me?

I said: "I don't know what Leonard is doing for you, and I didn't ask him, but I can tell you this: if he's worth $240 to you, I'm worth $2,400 because I'm ten times the man he is ever going to be."

Dead silence was all that came over the telephone. Then he said, "Are you putting me on?"

I said that I was not.

"Why don't you come down and see me?" he said.

One week later I was Leonard's boss.

11

Record-Keeping

Organized crime kills people and gets away with it, gets away with loan-sharking, narcotics trafficking, and all manner of illegal activities. Yet mob leaders get trapped on evasion of income taxes. Why? Because even the mob has to keep books. Nobody can keep the whole business in his head.

Records have to be kept. A flower retailer, for example, has to have a record of sales on such heavy volume days as Valentine's Day, Easter, and other holidays significant to that business. The retailer should know how many wreaths he bought the previous year at the same time and how many he sold, to help in his purchasing this time around. He may be able to remember for a while, but eventually all the Valentine's Days tend to run together. Many businesses ebb and increase with the seasons, or the time of day, or the day of the week. For the pool business, summer is the chemical sales season, and the operator should remember how many drums of water conditioner he bought the previous year. For a movie theater it's Saturday night. People buy more gasoline on Thursdays and Fridays, because they have just been paid.

Keeping track of such things is particularly important if, for instance, you have an ice cream parlor in South Dakota and just ran out of sundae dishes. It's going to be a problem finding a supplier in a hurry, and you may be out of business for a couple of days. The farther you are from your sources of supply, the more careful you must watch inventory.

For me at least, record-keeping is hardly the most fascinating part of operating a business. My temperament leads me to minimize it. The most important question of record-keeping is this: why am I keeping track of this? The answer may be that the government requires it, or it may be that it tells you something important about your business. If it meets neither of these two criteria, you should not be keeping the record.

As soon as I'm able to afford it and know what I'm doing, I turn the bulk of my record-keeping over to employees. Organizational skills just aren't my thing. I've tried to start files, putting things where they can be found, but it never works. The only answer is to have someone do it for me, even if it means giving up something somewhere else, or bringing in some extra money to pay for it. If it were up to me to keep records, my enterprise would become the *Titanic* of the business world—right to the bottom.

How Much Record-keeping?

Some people keep too many records and put too much energy into record-keeping. A temporary office personnel firm has computed that 65 cents of every dollar spent on filing is wasted, and that 85 percent of the documents filed are never looked at again. The problem with those figures, which I believe, is that you don't always know which documents will prove vitally important.

But you have to decide for yourself what you need, why you need it, and how it benefits you. The more complex your records, the more they can be messed up. Most people who begin keeping records make them too complex at first, and learn to streamline them only with experience. The best method is KISS: Keep It

Simple, Stupid. A number of standard record forms can be purchased at a stationery store. They are usually more complicated than they need to be, but as you gain experience they can be adapted to your own needs.

Simplicity is the thing. Get forty subdivisions down to three or four if that's all you need, with "Miscellaneous" filling in to cover a multitude of subjects. Don't inundate yourself with details. Why, for example, save all your bills? As long as you pay by check and annotate the check, it's all the record you need. Some people advise against that, because they fear that the IRS will say that you actually used the material for your house. I'm willing to take that chance rather than be buried in tons of paper that probably will baffle me if I try to find anything in it. On the other hand, you can probably devise some elaborate filing system that keeps everything accessible in seconds. This may cost more time and money than paying a penalty to the government. Even if a computer is used, it still takes time and manpower—and time is the one resource we never have enough of.

I have always stressed minimum records. For example, if a check comes in for the retail store, we just tear up our copy of the bill. There's no reason to keep a ledger on each person and their payments. On that rare occasion when somebody questions a bill, I'd rather give him the benefit of the doubt and pay the $20. It costs me a lot less than keeping voluminous records in which I prove that he never paid it.

For the big accounts, I'm a little more elaborate. When the check comes in it's posted. The check is compared to the bill to make sure that they correspond. A check mark is put in the ledger to show that this bill has been checked and the bill is moved to a dead file. As long as the bill is not in the dead file, it's outstanding. We rarely make mistakes that way, and it's simple. I don't understand why people get so involved in elaborate record systems. I once bought a book on how to keep records for a gas station; it convinced me that if I used that system, which I didn't, somebody would have to be writing down every time a sale was made. You can overrecord yourself.

Why You Need an Accountant

Some records have to be kept. Payroll records are essential not only to the government but to you. In most states, sales tax records are necessary; and because some items are subject to sales tax and others are not, these records are fairly complicated. Your records also must provide documentary proof that revenues stand at the level you claim. Most states also have a state income tax, and state income taxes have to be withheld, as do federal income taxes. If you have employees, you are required to contribute to the federal unemployment fund.

It's almost impossible for you to wade through this paper blizzard without an accountant. I have neither the space nor the competence to give you a definitive course in the intricacies of accounting. But let me just give you a bleak but sketchy idea of what awaits you:

If you have any employees, or engage any self-employed workers, you must have a federal tax number and a state tax number. You must file W-4 forms (for employees) and 1099s (for self-employed people) annually. You must file various reports with the federal government and the state over the course of the year—some semiannually, some quarterly, and some monthly. The dates on which these reports fall due come at various months and at various times of the month.

Throughout the year your accountant should take care of these matters and at the end of the year should file your annual statements, your personal income tax, and your other forms. Meanwhile your own energies should be directed to running the business, unless you're very good at such matters. Otherwise doing it yourself will not save you money but will cost you, because you will make mistakes, forget deadlines, etc.

Now that I've established the rule, let me suggest the exception. Even if you don't like keeping records, you ought to keep the sales tax records yourself, because nothing else can keep you up to date so well on what the business is grossing and thus give you a handle on how well it is doing. It is also a good idea to do the payroll yourself, including unemployment and social security records. I've always forced myself to do them. Thus every two weeks I can review who is working, how much they are making, and what has been the return on their labor.

I may see by these records that one of my employees has worked twenty hours of overtime over a two-week period. If I didn't do the payroll myself, I might not know until the end of the year that an employee has hundreds of hours of overtime. Then I would have to ask: why did we pay this employee all this overtime? But it would be too late to ask then. The overtime may be completely justified, but at least I get to ask about it every two weeks. I can see who's working overtime and what it's costing me. If the overtime is heavy, it might cost less to hire another person. If we need the extra work for only a week, however, and then don't need it for the following three weeks, the extra employee would not be justified. All this can easily be reviewed through payroll records. I could pay someone to do the payroll and make this review in some other way, but it does not take that long and it gives me a quick picture of what is happening.

Bookkeeping

Although you cannot and should not try to get along without an accountant, if you have a bent toward figures you can do the bookkeeping yourself. In fact at the beginning of your business you may have to. Accounting and bookkeeping are two different things.

It's best to have your accountant come in once a month, but sometimes once a quarter is enough. You will need a lot more from your accountant in initial services to help set up your system. He can establish the payroll sheets and then you only have to make the entries. Then the accountant can be called upon less often. But for the first few months at least he (or she, for there are lots of female accountants) should come in at least once a month, to critique your day-to-day records. If you wait three months for him to take the first look at them, it will be difficult to unscramble your mistakes.

As for posting, you can do that yourself, if you have the energy left to do it at the end of a long day. Obviously you should not be doing it during business hours, when your full attention should be directed to making your business thrive. Perhaps your spouse, or an older child, can do the bookkeeping. The more you do yourself, the less you have to pay an accountant.

Different kinds of enterprises call for different accounting procedures. If you're in a seasonal business, it may be to your advantage to use a fiscal year rather than a calendar year, since you may want to end your year at the end of your busy season. This would give you an advantage in catching up on record-keeping during the slack season. Most small businesses, however, tend to use the standard calendar year. Once you establish your accounting method the government is reluctant to let you change, so advance thinking is necessary. In some cases it might be easier—that is, might cause less governmental attention—to disband a corporation and start a new one with a different accounting method rather than try to change an established method.

Deductions

One thing your accountant and you will be talking over at tax time is deductions.

Take everything you can. Take your car, if you use it to do business. If you can find a good seminar that deals with your business, and it's in the Bahamas, nobody expects you to sit in your hotel room every minute that you're not at the seminar. Go to trade shows. If your spouse is active in the business as well, take him or her along.

If you have a good customer, there's nothing wrong with taking him out to dinner. It's expected. Your competition is going to do it.

One exception, though: I never claim my office-in-the-home as a tax deduction. How much is it worth? People with experience in tax matters will tell you that this is one of the things that the computer is keyed to spit out. Suppose the IRS audits my return because of an office in the home. It would cost me more to send my accountant to the IRS office for the audit than it would benefit me for the next three or four years. I'm not telling you not to do it, however; you should rely heavily on your accountant's advice on that one.

Sometimes the IRS raises questions about whether you are actually in business at all. This happens more often when you have a regular W-4 job and also work at your own business. What you are attempting to show the IRS is that you are really trying to make a profit—not trying to create deductions or trying to make a hobby look like a business.

If you're going door-to-door trying to sell a product, it's unlikely that the IRS will respond, "Boy, that's a nice hobby you've got there." But if your business is building model airplanes and trying to sell them to restaurants as decor, you may find the IRS skeptical about the seriousness of your business.

As in the case with the office-in-the-home, is it worth an IRS audit to save a few dollars in deductions? First of all, it's unlikely that you can handle it; maybe you can, but I can't. I can't talk the language of the IRS; I'd send my accountant. So that costs me money to begin with.

With the IRS, I keep a dollar figure in mind; anything it wants that comes in under that figure, I just pay it. The IRS says I owe them $89; I just send the check. It costs me more money to find out that I *don't* owe them the $89. Some people argue that it's better to stand up and be counted. That means saving $89 and sending the accountant a check for $200. Somehow I don't see that as a victory. So I pay the IRS, not because I tried to cheat the government or because I think the IRS is right. It's the same as a parking ticket for $10. I've paid a lot of tickets in my life although I knew that the meter was broken, but it wasn't worth my while to sit five hours in a court to get my case dismissed. I operate the same way with the IRS. If the IRS came up with big numbers, however, that would be another story.

Inventory

Keeping inventory records does not involve just what you buy and sell, but also when you buy and sell as well. In the toy business, you may sell most of them in November and December, but you buy them in February. Before you buy toys you need to know about the manufacturer's marketing plans. You have every right to ask how much he's going to spend on advertising, as well as where the advertising will appear. Otherwise how do you know what to buy? In the toy business what is advertised is what sells.

Sometimes supply doesn't depend on the season but on the time of the month. A retailer in a heavy welfare area would gear his purchasing to the arrival of welfare checks, when the volume of purchasing will greatly increase.

Your inventory records should also keep you abreast of what is selling and what is not. A decade ago a flower store couldn't keep hanging baskets in stock; customers would buy them as you walked in the door with them. That was the era of the plant; some plant stores didn't even sell flowers. Nowadays people still buy plants, but not with the fervor that they bought them in the days of love beads. Although the rose is always with us, some flowers sell for a season or two and then yield their popularity to another.

The retailer has to have a handle on these changes and records help considerably. In the case of plants, you can't grow something in a few hours, so you have to have some advance knowledge. But that's true in most businesses; the clothing store has committed itself to the fall fashions long before they show up in the windows. If people want something that you can't supply, that's terrible for business.

Records Help in Many Ways

Suppose you have a little snack shop and a big parade is coming up. It sounds like a lot of business for you. But on parade day there may be forty-five vending trucks outside your door competing with you. You have to anticipate what is going to happen, and records help you do that.

If an item of merchandise sells in a certain season, what did you pay for it last year, how did you price it, and what did you have to throw away? If you bought one hundred of them and only sold ninety, you have to increase your cost per item. Let's say you paid one dollar for each and sold them for two dollars each. You think you made one dollar on each but your records will show you that you only made 90 cents each. Why? Because ten of them were thrown away, making your real price $1.10 each. You may also have bought one hundred of an item and sold them all, but had to mark some of them down to sell them. That may not be in your head, but it's in your records.

The complexion of an area changes with time. You think your business is the same yesterday, today, and tomorrow, but maybe the area was rural a decade ago and now has become quite suburbanized. And the suburban customer differs from the rural customer. Or perhaps the customers have become older—maybe just through time, or maybe because there's now a retirement community nearby.

If you're in the grocery business, that will probably make a difference in what you sell—and in what sizes you sell. Older people buy in smaller sizes. A widow, living alone, is not going to buy the big economy size of baked beans. She's looking for the smallest size. City stores, because of the larger percentage of single people in cities, tend to stock small sizes, while suburban stores, selling to the family with four children, stock more large sizes. Not, however, if a lot of the customers live in a retirement community. So you have to keep track of all those factors. Do your customers tend to drive up or walk up? If they walk, probably they want smaller sizes.

Records can be used to keep your employees honest. One ice cream business doesn't keep track of ice cream but keeps close watch over the containers. If two hundred containers are gone there had better be money in the drawer for two hundred pints of ice cream. Broken unusable cones have to be saved. Of course the employees can beat this system if they try hard; there's no system that can't be beaten. But if the people working for you know these things are working, it gives them some pause. I'll have more to say about insuring honesty in a later chapter.

I always kept track of a number of oddball indicators. When I was in the summer camp business I could tell you on April 1, within a percentage point, how many kids we'd have in camp that year. So by that date I knew what we'd need in groceries, staff, and on down the line.

I had a graph made of how many people were signed up by then, and the curve always showed the same percentage of the total every year. I used the April 1 date because we gave an early discount. So, if you have such an indicator, and by the middle of March you see that business is off, maybe you had better make a move—start or increase advertising, or something.

The small computer has already begun to make a great difference in record-keeping. To give you a wacky analogy: one way to cook is to wash each pot as you go along, since you're in the kitchen anyway. The other is to keep using pots, pile them up, and then wash them when the cooking is over. The computer lets you keep records the first way, as you go along. Everything is registered as it happens, so that you are up-to-date minute by minute. As computer use spreads, that will become the norm. Today's computers are cheap and user-friendly, and your competitors are going to be using them, so you should be using one too. In a few years even local candy stores will keep track of inventory with computers.

Many enterprises, such as pharmacies, already do all of their ordering by computer. When the pharmacist sees that he is down to the next-to-last bottle of a product, he just goes to the telephone, dials the number of the computer at his wholesaler's, and punches in the proper code number.

Remember that in a beginning business your margin for error is small. A couple of mistakes and it's all over. That's why keeping a sharp eye on the records is particularly important at the outset.

12

Buying and Pricing

BUYING

Front Door and Back Door

There are some things you can't control in business and other things you can. That holds true whether you're the elderly lady with the card shop or the hairy ham-fisted fellow renting heavy equipment.

You can try advertising, solicitation, price-cutting, and all sorts of strategems to try to influence sales, but beyond a certain point it either happens or it doesn't—the sales come or they don't.

But there is another side to the business, and over this side you have firm control, and that's the matter of how you spend what comes in. There's so much concentration on the front door (what's coming in) that business people often overlook their control over the back door (what's going out).

Buying Smart

Take advantage of the discounts available in buying in large quantities. If you think that the price is too high, stop and do the arithmetic, and you may find that you can't afford not to. You'll never find an investment that will bring you the interest, and you'll never find the hungriest loan-shark charging the interest that equals such a discount. When a supplier offers to give you ten cases free if you buy a hundred cases, figure that discount out, and you'll see it's enormous.

Not long ago the fellow who runs a business we own bought forty cases of something we needed. "Forty cases!" I exclaimed. "Where are we going to store forty cases?"

"I got it," he said, "for $14.50 a case. The stuff usually sells for $21.50 a case."

"Find a place to store it," I said.

Unless you're sitting at the corner of Fifth Avenue and Fifty-fifth Street in New York, where a square foot of storage space is so expensive that nobody can afford it, it pays to buy in quantity. If it's not perishable and you can forecast your needs, buying for a year is not unreasonable.

Another great saving can be accomplished by cutting out one level of handling. Buy at the source if you can. Sometimes that isn't easy, because the manufacturers are afraid that wholesalers will object. The problem with buying direct from the manufacturer is three-fold: first, to find him, which is often difficult; second, to persuade him to sell to you; and third, to be able to buy in a quantity that makes it worthwhile. Even if you have to borrow from a bank at 20 percent interest, buying wholesale may keep you ahead of the game. It even pays to buy or rent more warehouse space.

Another money-saver: some firms offer a 2 percent discount if the bill is paid within ten days. Let's say the bill is for $1,000. Your reaction may be that it's a lot of money to come up with right away.

Now, if you went to a bank and were offered a loan at 35 percent, you'd wonder if Jesse James had decided to work the other side of banks for a while. But what does 2 percent for ten days work out to? Remember, you don't have to pay on the first day, but on the tenth. So you're only getting another twenty days to pay it anyway. By paying the bill on the tenth day you have saved $20 for twenty days, which works out to $365 a year. That's better interest than they're asking at the Jesse James National Bank. So if you don't discount your bills, you're not taking advantage of an edge.

Frequently companies will discount only if you ask. So you should give it a try. The worst that can happen is a smile that says, "Don't be ridiculous." And having asked, you have put your supplier on the spot, and it's his move. Maybe he thinks another widget salesman has approached you and offered a discount. Therefore, without expecting to, he may agree to your suggestion. Some companies do not discount but will give you extra merchandise for prompt payment. Some companies even offer a further discount of one percent if you pay cash on delivery; they call it "anticipation." Ask—it never hurts to ask.

Forming buying cooperatives is another way to save money in buying. Many retailers have joined them. If you as a relatively small appliance store owner buy four washing machines every quarter, General Electric is not going to look at you as an important customer. But if you get together with a hundred other appliance store owners, all relatively noncompetitive, and pool your purchases, you'll be dealing with GE from a position of strength.

On a nondiscounted bill your policy should be to pay as late as possible. The electric company is periodically threatening to turn off my lights because I pay late.

"Why do I have to keep calling you to pay your bills?" a utility company representative asked me one day.

"When you start discounting," I replied, "you won't have to call anymore. Until you start discounting, I'm going to use your money right up to the last possible day. I know you guys do the same thing." He admitted as much. I see nothing wrong in using their money that way; they've lent me money involuntarily, just as I am an involuntary lender to many of my customers. If I can defer payment for a month, in effect I have borrowed that money for a month for nothing.

Telephone Costs

My telephone bills approach the debts of small nations. Nevertheless I try to get every advantage I can. There are so many choices in telephone systems these days, both among competing companies and among a variety of choices in a company, that some big corporations have specialists who do nothing else. Obviously you can't devote all your time to telephone systems, but it's undoubtedly worth your time to look into the various offers to get the best buy at the best price for you.

Choosing a long distance company involves many factors. Do they charge by the split minute, or by the minute? Do you get instant credit for a wrong number? Do you pay for a call if you allow the phone to ring more than six times? The system that's best for my business may not be best for yours, and the differences may be considerable. You also have to determine how much quality you will pay a premium for. In some businesses the quality of transmission is vital; in others it's relatively unimportant.

Inventory

The amount of inventory you need varies enormously depending on the kind of business you are in. A hardware store carries a staggering inventory. People expect you to have anything they may ask for, even if no one else has asked for it in two years. On the other end of the scale, an ice-cream shop can chug along on a low inventory outlay; a thousand dollars buys a lot of ice cream, and often the company selling you the ice cream will provide you with the cabinets. Fudge also is situated at the low end of the inventory scale; if you plan to open a fudge shop, remember that a thousand dollars buys a lot of fudge and that it lacks a long shelf life. (It is recyclable, however; fudge can easily be melted down and used again.)

Some businesses are so inventory-heavy that you have to floor-plan the operation. ("Floor-planning" is an insider phrase meaning finance your inventory—that is, the bank owns everything in your showroom.) Used-car lots, an operation heavy in inventory, are invariably floor-planned. A forty-car used-car lot, which is rather modest in size, at an average value of $5,000 per car, comes to $200,000 in inventory. Many small businesspeople can't hope to own that much inventory outright. They floor-plan the inventory all the way through the life of the business. If this is true in your case, and if you never get out of debt so far as your inventory is concerned, remember to factor your interest charges into your overhead.

Good retailers do not let inventory sit. They know it is taking up good $15-per-square foot space, so they move it. If they made a bad buy they get it out. Sell it at cost, sell it at a loss, but get rid of it. Filene's in Boston, the store with the famous basement, knows that space is money, so if it doesn't sell in a certain number of days, they move it out. Some retailers move everything around every three weeks, even from one counter to another, so it looks as though the merchandise is moving.

PRICING

Price is a direct consequence of buying, and so buying is often the key to success in business. The people who can work on a very close profit margin in retailing are the people who buy right, who take advantage of every opportunity in discounting and in buying bargains.

Knowing what to charge can be difficult. It causes business people hours of thought and rethinking.

I have a friend in the contracting business who says that when he's done pricing he adds another 10 percent. That surcharge, he said, usually does not amount to a bonanza of extra profit; it's usually eaten up by mistakes and unforeseen costs.

Bakeries often figure their price as one-third for cost of materials, one-third for labor, and one-third for profit. That formula seems to work for bakers, but other trades are not that easy to factor. The company that converts a pound of steel into a pound of delicate springs clearly has little use for the bakery formula. The artist who takes a stretched canvas and a few dollars worth of paint and creates a painting obviously has to use a formula that differs from the baker's.

For all the hours that businesspeople spend worrying about overpricing, the major problem for most of them is underpricing. They persuade themselves that they can make a profit at a certain price and overlook various items of expense. Insurance costs only a few dollars a day but a few dollars times 365 is a lot of money annually, and must be factored into the price. Many people fail to realize that the time they spend talking to a client should be figured in the price; if a baker puts in an hour talking to a customer about a special cake, that's an hour of work time.

A fellow went into the business of videotaping the complete interior of homes as a registration of possessions for fire or theft insurance. He was charging $25 an hour. When he called me, I suggested that he'd soon go under at that price. The costs of his time and equipment just would not allow a profit. Yet to him it seemed a lot of money.

Another caller was a woman woodworker. The material for a shelf she was making cost about $25. She put about ten hours of work into it and was adding $5 for delivery. She asked me how much she ought to charge. "Let me guess what you're selling it for—about $75," I said.

"That's right," she said.

"And you ought to be selling it for $140," I said.

"You're kidding!" she responded.

Most of us tend to undervalue our services, and artistic and crafts people do this more so than the average. If you have a great problem, as is true of many artistic types, in dealing with pricing, you ought to have a number-oriented business manager running your business for you.

I understand the reluctance to raise prices. Every time I raise prices I look at the situation forty different ways, and raise them hesitantly. But I never price against competition; if someone else can undersell me, I just don't have the answer to that. Pricing against competition is what sent the airlines into a tailspin.

I sell to hospitals in my wholesale flower business, giving a percentage of the gross to the hospital, and it's exactly the same with each hospital. One of the bigger hospitals tumbled into considerable financial trouble not long ago and asked me to give an extra 15 percent. I could not profitably do it. "If I give it to you," I told the hospital administrator, "I've got to give the same to the other hospitals." We were doing a lot of business with that hospital, and we lost the account. A similar series of events occurred with another hospital. I was sorry to lose them, but we could not produce the goods at that level of quality and give up another 15 percent. They found someone else to do it for them. I don't know how; it was probably by lowering the quality of goods. The hospital told me that my competition was doing it, and I don't doubt it, but how long can they do it? We're making a profit and most of our customers are happy. Why screw that up to keep two accounts that I might lose anyway, especially if the hospitals are in such sorry financial shape?

I don't make special deals. If two of my customers ever get together and compare notes, one will never find that he is paying more, or less, than another. Some people make a legitimate case for volume, that a fellow who gives you ten times as much volume ought to get a better price. That's probably true in some businesses, but I've never found it so in any of my own. I don't see any difference in costs, and I think not making deals has stood me in good stead.

Turnover a Factor

Pricing depends on turnover. In a supermarket you might possibly make only one percent profit, but the volume makes up for it. The goods are gone in a week, or should be at such a low profit margin. In a gift shop goods turn over only about twice a year, and in a furniture store only once. In the jewelry business a brooch may sit on the shelf for years, and it costs money to keep it sitting there all that time.

Sometimes the market just makes profit on some items impossible. A service station operates on an impossibly slim profit margin for gasoline and makes its profit on tires, batteries, and repairs. Nevertheless the stuff in the ground has to be paid for.

Reducing Overhead

Overhead figures heavily in pricing. A fudge kiosk that rents for $100 a square foot is obviously a heavier factor than an out-of-the-way restaurant that rents for two dollars a square foot.

But even though rent is a fixed expense, you can affect the ratio of rent to volume, and of other fixed expenses to volume. Except for gasoline and other operating prices, your fleet costs the same no matter how much or how little you use it. The trucks are going to turn to rust at the same rate whether you use them eight hours a day or sixteen hours. The tires may go faster, but the truck body will be doing the work of two eight-hour-a-day trucks.

If you stay open longer hours you may not only increase sales by 50 percent, but you may also reduce your merchandise cost by 10 percent because you will be buying in greater bulk. If you go from a six-days-a-week operation to seven, you may not find the seventh day profitable in itself, but it may make the other days profitable. Your customers on the seventh day may be only marginally profitable but you will generate more overall profit because you can buy at greater volume. The fast-food franchises went into the breakfast business because they could open more hours per day and thus do more volume with the same fixed rent expense.

Billing

The trick is . . . don't bill. Get cash if you can. Accept credit cards if possible. A Visa or MasterCard is just like cash. Don't have any accounts receivable if you can avoid them. Get the money up front.

But sometimes that's too expensive. Take a wholesale business. If you have your driver collect when he makes a delivery, he has to wait around while the customer counts the money or comes up with the checkbook, and meanwhile that expensive truck is sitting outside.

Minor credit is a big problem, and retailers are getting away from it. It costs you a dollar to send out a bill. On a $10 purchase there is no profit in it. And that's assuming that your debtor will send you the $10 back. If he doesn't, you send out a second bill and spend another buck.

If somebody owes you a lot of money, you can go after him, but how do you collect $30? The answer is, you don't. You give it to a collection agency and hope it can get you $15. How much time can you afford to spend trying to collect $30? A lawyer will laugh at you. He'll shoot off one letter, possibly, on your behalf. If you're a good client he has to accommodate you. If he gets no response, that's the end of it. You can't go to Small Claims Court for the money; your time is worth more than that. And what happens if you do get a judgment in your favor? Try collecting it.

Business people worry a lot about bad checks, yet I've never found them much of a problem. Of course I've gotten an occasional one, but over the course of a year they don't add up to a lot of money. The same is true with bad credit cards. Some retailers call at a certain limit; below that, the credit card company guarantees payment. Credit has always been a bigger problem than bad checks and cards.

Yet I couldn't advise you not to extend credit. There are advantages to a charge account. It induces the customer to buy with you instead of elsewhere. Department stores figure a credit card is worth $50 to them. Frequently if a customer is in a mall and has a credit card for one store, that's the one he heads for.

Charge interest on late bills. Notify people at the bottom of a second notice that you are charging one and a half percent per month in interest. I do it. If somebody decides not to pay the interest, I don't do anything about it, but that's the end of their credit.

With big debtors, work with them, bring them along and get them paid up, if you want to keep them as customers. With small debtors, don't get too involved because it isn't worth your time. One day when I was in a bad mood I took my son Matthew out with me knocking on the doors of people who owed me money. We collected about $500 in an afternoon. Some said they couldn't pay the whole $30 but could give us $10 and we took it, and never approached them again for the rest.

You ought to make up-front payment, in whole or in part, a policy in some businesses. Certainly if you're a baker, and a stranger walks in and orders a very special cake, you ought to have the money up front. Custom orders of any sort should be paid for in advance.

Installment payments are customary in some businesses. But don't forget that when money is coming in a little at a time that you are in effect extending credit, and your prices should reflect that.

Credit Cards

Some businesses are able to thrive without credit cards. A restaurant will hang up a "No Credit Cards" sign, and people continue standing in line to get in. That's only because they have good food. Even then the restaurant is kicking away some business, because many corporate executives will not spend cash. Sending in an expense voucher based on a credit card is easy, but sending in a voucher on a cash purchase is difficult.

The credit card has become central to our system not only because it eliminates the need to carry cash but because it establishes credit-worthiness—it is widely used for that purpose, especially at hotels—and can be used to take out small loans without seeing a bank or loan company.

Thus credit cards have become a permanent factor in our economy. Yet they carry a price for the retailer. When you accept credit cards you are giving up part of your net—anywhere from 4 percent for a small business to 1.5 percent for a big business. Therefore if you have a small business and work on a very tight profit margin, the credit card may be unacceptable at 4 percent, whereas in a high-ticket business at 1.5 percent it's a negligible factor. Many service stations, for example, operate on a slim profit margin for gasoline. If a driver pays by credit card for gas, the 3 percent rate may completely wipe out profit.

If you don't accept credit cards but decide as an alternative to establish your own charge system, this will also cost money—probably more money. You will have to bill people every month, and process what comes in, and figure that you will get an occasional deadbeat. So your own charge system will raise costs, and that will have to be factored into your prices.

Visa and MasterCard, the two largest credit-card operations, operate through individual banks and other institutions. The next largest card companies, American Express, the Discover Card, and Diner's Club, operate otherwise. The advantage of the bank cards to the merchant is quick cash-in; he or she can run over to the bank with the receipts and quickly convert them to money. The non-bank cards tie up your money for longer periods, but the longer they keep your money the lower the rate you have to pay.

American Express offers you a couple of options. If you want to get paid right away you pay a higher percentage charge than if you are willing to wait and be paid once a month. This is offered at a lower rate because it saves American Express paperwork and gives them the use of your money for a float of a few days.

There's another option open for small businesspeople. There are clearing houses, usually in a trade association of some kind, that will take all your charge card business. You send the slips to the clearing house, and its staff will do all the sorting and send you a statement. Naturally there is a charge for this, and the clearing house has your money for a while. But you don't have to do all the sorting, sending this one to Visa, this one to American Express, and the next someplace else. You just pop it to the clearing house in an envelope. It saves you a lot of paperwork. Of course, if you are working really tight, you may not be able to stand being separated from your money for that long.

Sometimes little businesses will do better with banks if they band together in an association. Even the little individual businesses can talk with the bank for a better rate, however, because everything is negotiable. The negotiation leverage you have is volume and ticket price, and of the two the latter is more important. If you gross a million dollars in credit card sales annually and they average five dollars per sale, you are not that attractive to the bank and your rate will be higher. If you are grossing the same volume annually and your average sale is $200, the bank finds that attractive and may offer a lower rate. The higher-ticket business moves the same amount of money through the bank in far fewer transactions, and transactions cost the bank money.

If you decide to accept plastic you must determine what percentage of your business you expect via credit card. If very high (such as a restaurant with 95 percent credit-card business) you have to build the three or four percent rate into your pricing as another cost of doing business. But if your credit-card share of the gross is small, you may safely disregard it. For example, if your business grosses $500,000 annually and only 2 percent of that gross comes from credit-card business, that amounts (based on a 1.5 percent credit-card bank rate) to only $300 in annual bank charges.

If tips are included on a credit card, you have to decide whether or not to discount the employee's tip. On a $20 tip, 60 cents (on a 3 percent credit card rate) will go to bank charges. Does the waiter's tip get reduced to $19.40, or does the owner eat the difference? Unless you discount from the beginning, you may have an employee revolt on your hands if you try to change the rules in your favor later.

13

Marketing

There's a hamburger place I love. The man who owns the place is always in the back making hamburgers. He has a speech impediment. He thinks people mock him, so he has problems dealing with the public. So he stays behind the scenes. Yet the place is always full of customers. Not one of the people who work for him could have made it into the success that he has, because that success called for a number of diverse skills. The one skill he lacks is meeting the public, so he delegates that job.

Everybody knows the example of the merchant who was so good that even though you had to wait in line, and his prices were higher, and he didn't even bother to be nice to you everybody went there anyway. They stood cheerfully in line because he made the best strudel in town, or the best homemade ice cream. If you are really good, people are probably going to find you, eventually. People like this may not need to worry about marketing. But it is rare that a businessperson does not have to make a major effort to market properly.

Salesmanship

If you're a retailer, marketing may just mean putting up the right sign. If you're a wholesaler, it may just mean placing the right calls.

On the other hand, you may have to sell your product or service. Salesmen are necessary in some businesses even if they are mostly order-takers, because if they don't make the calls your competitor will walk through the door and take the order.

If you are a wholesale shortening salesman, is there any question when you walk into a bakery that the baker needs shortening? Of course he does. Your job is to persuade him to buy *your* shortening. The job of the salesman is to cultivate the baker, to establish a relationship with him, as well as to give him a little break on terms and see that the goods are delivered on time and that he is satisfied.

There are other salesmen who are more than order-takers. The customer didn't know until the salesman walked in that he needed the product. The salesman created that need. That's true marketing in my estimate.

Let me tell you something, however, that I've never heard said anywhere else: of all the mistakes businesspeople make, salesmanship is probably where the fewest errors are made. That's because most businesspeople put so much emphasis and thinking into it. There's no question that you have to sell your product. But if I had to put my best employee in sales or in purchasing, I'd put him in purchasing. Much less emphasis is put upon it, yet it's vital.

Creative Marketing

Frequently if you're in business you will be approached for charitable contributions, and often they involve golf tournaments. You get your name on a hole of the course for something like $750. One merchant didn't want to spend that much money just to have his name on a sign with a lot of other people. So he offered $10,000 for a hole-in-one on the ninth hole. The offer got his picture in the newspaper with a huge check eight feet long, but he only had to spend $450 for an insurance policy that would pay the $10,000 if anyone scored a hole-in-one, so he saved $300 and upstaged everybody else. That's marketing.

An appliance store merchant had a nice showroom, so a lot of people would come in to look. Then they would go down the street to a discount store to compare prices. Now how did he deal with that? Everybody who came in to look at the appliances was given free ice cream. The shoppers didn't want the ice cream to melt, so they took the ice cream right home.

Actually that trick originated with real estate people. If you have an open house and you don't want the couples going next to your competitors, you give them ice cream as they leave. If I were the competitor, I'd be outside with spoons and napkins, advising them to eat the ice cream and come look at some great houses.

Here's a gimmick for the flower business: at Easter have all the delivery men and the clerks dress in bunny costumes. A customer may go into ten stores that day, but that night when she's talking with her friends, that's the store she'll talk about.

Gimmicks pay in that sense, but there's a problem with them. They just get the public's attention. You can sell the squeal but you've got to deliver a pig. And if you don't then you may have made an enemy. Cute, but no substance—that will be the line on your business.

With imagination, though, there are many ways you can promote on just a small budget. You can outdo the big companies on gimmickry because they have to hold six meetings, get fourteen vice presidents to agree on it, and then wait to see what the head man thinks of it.

Advertising

To advertise properly you have to find the right medium. It varies tremendously from one enterprise to another. In automobile rental, it was the Yellow Pages. A high percentage of our business came from there. That's also true of plumbers, extermi-nators, and most repair-type enterprises. That's where the cus-tomer looks. But I don't see the Yellow Pages as nearly as important for a small retailer. If you're looking to buy a dress or go out to eat, do you consult the Yellow Pages? Maybe to find the address, but not to make a decision.

When we ran the auto rental we had good results with radio advertising, but we found that newspaper advertising didn't bring any response. Yet radio advertising didn't sell our summer camp; newspaper advertising worked a lot better. We discovered that neither radio nor newspaper advertising sold flowers. Nothing sells our flowers more than the big sign outside offering a dozen roses for $15. But the only people who see it are people who pass by. Most people are not going to drive ten miles to buy a dozen roses, even at a good price. Why does one medium work and another not work? The pragmatic answer is, I don't care why. This one works and this one doesn't.

There's no question that advertising sells. If you spend enough on advertising, you will sell something. Whether you will sell enough to make it worth the cost of the advertising is something else again. That's the kind of numbers that you have to discover to find the right advertising for your business. Every smart businessman tracks his business to find out where it's coming from—radio, newspaper, consumers' periodicals like the *Pennysaver*, direct mail, flyers on car windshields, word of mouth, special offers, special sales, coupons, or whatever.

The Right Copy

I talked to a woman who had what she thought was going to be a good business. Essentially she would be a glorified errand girl. She would shop for the busy executive, get an anniversary present for his wife, remember her birthday and so on. She had brochures printed up and sent out two thousand. She did not get a single reply.

Obviously she had done something wrong. Even if you're in Alaska selling ice to the Eskimos, you ought to get at least one reply in two thousand entries; that's only one-twentieth of one percent. There could be lots of reasons why this brochure flopped, from being sent to the wrong list of people all the way to the printed material itself. To my mind the trouble was the brochure. It was too verbose, and few people would bother to read it. It should have tried to do less and supplied a number that people could call for more information. Which letters do you read in the letters to the editor column? The ones a whole column long, or the short, punchy ones?

I'm constantly going through this problem with my radio advertisers. They want to put the whole Bible into a sixty-second commercial. That's not effective. In an advertisement you focus on one aspect of your business that makes it appealing. It might be price, quality, or location—the reason why people should want to do business with you. But most advertisers don't know that. They try to cram too much into an ad, and nobody pays attention.

Ready for Departure

Beginners in business have another common attitude that only wears away with time. They run an advertisement three times and expect to see customers rocketing through the door. But it's repetition that makes an ad successful, the same message over and over and over.

I'll tell you a personal experience that underlines that for me. This happened in a different age—the early 1950s—when people didn't fly everywhere the way they do now. My best friend was getting married and asked me to be best man. The wedding was in New Jersey and I was stationed in Texas. Now today nobody thinks twice about jumping on a plane and flying across the continent for the day and then flying back. But in 1951 people didn't do that.

211

I used to hear this commercial on the radio every morning: "Eastern Airlines now ready for departure." That was the whole commercial, at least in essence. Now I have to make the first airline reservation I've ever made. In those days you called the airport and they switched you to the airline you wanted. Now I'm anxious not to appear stupid when I call the airport. So when I was asked which airline I wanted, what do you suppose I said? Of course I said "Eastern Airlines." It was the only airline I had ever heard of.

Beer companies operate on the same premise. Nobody wants to look dumb at the bar. When the bartender asks you what you want, you can't just say you want a beer. You have to say some brand, or you'll look like a monkey. So you think of a brand quick—the one that's been hammering its name into your skull day after day. Beer commercials don't say anything about how good the beer is. They just keep mentioning the brand name. So unless you are really established as the drinker of a particular brand, that's the one you say when you're asked.

Now that kind of saturation advertising is expensive. But that is how it works. We found that you have to advertise continuously.

The mainstay of my retail flower and plant store is the sign outside that offers a dozen roses for $15. We have developed a reputation for selling roses at a good, low price. It took us a decade to develop that—ten years of selling at about a third to a half of our competition's prices. Take that sign down and in two days business drops off 75 percent.

Why? How can you determine why people don't come in? Maybe they think we have raised the price of roses. Or that we are out of roses. Or maybe it takes the sign to remind them to buy roses. Or maybe it is a combination of all these. Whatever the reason, business plummets instantly into an abyss.

That's why these beer companies keep banging away. Because the public has a memory shorter than anyone can believe and very little loyalty to a brand.

Yellow Pages

In a crisis, the Yellow Pages is the first place we look. We also tend to look there for a product that we don't regularly use. You don't rent a chain saw often, but when you do, you probably check the Yellow Pages. But if you need a gallon of milk, do you look up "Milk Stores" in the Yellow Pages?

It's a mistake to try to get a dissertation into a Yellow Pages ad. It should give readers two or three very quick ideas, not lines of fine print. Although you may be fascinated with the fourteen different kinds of grain leather you have for sale in your luggage store, that isn't the place to go into them.

If you're going into a business that ought to depend heavily on Yellow Pages, you ought to look ahead. Find out when the Yellow Pages closes for your area. If you don't check, you could face a very lean eleven months until you get into the next year's edition. I have a closing list for the state of New Jersey and as I have looked for new locations in which to place an ad, I've referred to the list. If making a choice between the Jones County and the Smith County books, we may put the business in Smith County because its closing date for the Yellow Pages is sooner.

The Yellow Pages pays, but it's become expensive over recent years. And if you both sell luggage and repair luggage, you have to think about cross-listing. There may be two sections of the Pages for these two specialties, and perhaps you should be in both.

It seems to me that the Yellow Pages have worked out their directories so that you have to appear in two or even three directories to be noticed by all the potential customers in your area. But I don't blame them for that; I'd probably do the same thing.

The Advertising Dollar

Executives in big companies agonize and analyze about where to spend advertising money. And the market is more fragmented than ever. Radio has talk-show stations, and black stations, and various subdivisions of rock music, and easy listening, and clas-

sical music stations, and country and western. You don't advertise pimple cream on the classical music station. If you're selling
Afro-Sheen, you advertise on the black station. It's the same in
small business and, as in big business, it's a mistake to try to get it
all. The Second Coming of Christ would probably only get
about an 80 percent market share.

If you have a pizza parlor in New York City or Chicago, it's too
expensive to advertise on local radio. You're paying for a broadcast signal that goes much too far for your little neighborhood
business. The same is true for some newspapers. But a little local
radio station or newspaper may be just right for you. Some cable
television stations are now offering local spots; you can put your
advertisement on local TV at a moderate price.

Placement gets even more finely tuned than that. If you are
running a display advertisement in a newspaper, where do you
want it? Some pages cost more than others. You'll be advised that
if it's a product for men, put it on the sports pages. But many
potential male customers never look at sports pages.

Merchandising

The game of in-store merchandising is to get your customers
to buy something they didn't come in for. In the supermarket
business that's what front-end displays are about. For impulse
buying, the closer to the cash register the better. On the down
side, however, that also makes it the easiest stolen.

I will never be able to understand the psychology of pricing
something at $4.99 instead of at $5. The same penny that the
customer wouldn't deign to pick up if he saw it lying on the
sidewalk is thought to help sell the item because at five dollars
there is sales resistance but not at four dollars plus change. So
don't reinvent the wheel. If it works, do it; and this seems to
work. Look at gasoline stations; instead of just knocking off one
penny they knock off one-tenth of a penny.

Sales

They are so often just abused. Yet the public seems to want to be fooled. The proof: there are just too many successful retailers who advertise sales all the time and make money at it.

Other Gimmicks

Here's another gimmick that we tried, and it worked. Everybody said it wouldn't. We had scrip printed that was given to a customer for every sale. It represented 5 percent of the sale—so if a customer spent ten dollars, he received 50 cents worth of scrip. He had to come back another time to use it. It was amazing. People would drive ten miles to cash in 50 cents worth of scrip. The customer couldn't save up enough scrip to get something free; it could only be applied to the next sale. It brought in a lot of return customers.

A pharmacy I know of offers something of the same kind of deal using sales register tapes. The owner deducts 10 percent of the amount of the tapes toward a purchase by cash or check. His basic aim is not so much to bring in return customers, as to induce people to pay at once instead of running up a charge, as so many people do in pharmacies. Not only does this eliminate waiting for his money, but also cuts the expense of sending out monthly bills and reduces the number of bad accounts that fail to pay up.

There's a bar way out west where the drinks are served in Mason jars. They're so big you can almost jump in and swim around. That's not for me—I'd prefer a smaller drink and a better glass—but it apparently works. I know of some stores that use newspaper to wrap packages; it's a kind of signature that makes them distinctive. I know of a gift shop that attracts customers not because of its rather ordinary merchandise, but because when a package is gift wrapped there it's outstandingly done. The paper, the box, the ribbon all make a big impression.

We all know of stores that come to mind with a glance at the distinctive wrapping.

Cleanliness

Psychologically, customers are more likely to come to a pleasant place with ordinary merchandise than to an awful place with great merchandise—particularly if being a customer involves staying in the place, as in a restaurant. So cleanliness is a big item in merchandising—although some saloons make their reputation by keeping two inches of peanut shells on the floor.

From the Customer's View

Get them waited on and get them out. People do not like to wait in line. So many stores err in this. You walk into a hardware store and the clerk is talking to a customer about a couple of washers. You stand and wait and wait. The clerk could interrupt this ongoing discussion to ask you if he can be of help. Understandably, the other person is a customer too, but often won't mind helping you get out fast. When I go into a store and find myself waiting, it's a while before I go back again.

If I had one phrase I could erase from a clerk's vocabulary it would be this: "Is that it?" It's a big turnoff. A positive phrase would be: "Will there be something else?"

Customers also don't want to hear clerks bitching. How many times have you been to a store where the clerk has something negative to say about his job?

Two Merchandising Approaches

If you know that you just want to sell 10,000 shares of AT&T stock, there's no reason in the world to go to a full-service broker. Why should you pay a full-service commission when all you want is an execution? You can shop around for the cheapest discount broker.

The employer doesn't have to have a really savvy guy at a discount brokerage house. All he has to do is pick up the telephone and execute the order. The full-service broker, on the other hand, has to be able to say: "I'm not sure it's a good idea for you to sell right now. Our research shows that AT&T may advance two or three points in the next couple of weeks. If you can borrow money instead of selling the stock it might be worth a lot of money to you."

In the second instance, at the full-service house, you're going to pay more commission fees.

Those are the two basic ways to merchandise. Say you want to buy a VCR, and all you know about them is that they record television shows and play tapes. If you walk into a full-service operation the employee will explain to you how they work, what advantages this one has over that, and which you ought to buy based on what you are looking for. In the discount house the employee says: "This one is 299 bucks. That one is 399 bucks."

The average Yuppie doesn't really need a full-service store. He has already done the research on what he needs, what he wants, and how much the things he wants cost. But if you're like me, you're concerned about turning on the VCR when it's in the attack mode. I don't have a clue about what I'm buying, and I'm better off going into the full-service place where I will get all the help I need.

The customer who buys in the full-service store often can't handle a discount store. He gets lost, he can't pull the items off the shelf, he's frustrated at standing in line at a checkout counter with his birth certificate and two other documents of identification before they'll take his charge card. He's used to the high-class place where the employee says, "Of course we'll take a personal check."

Those are two different approaches. In the high-class place they will take a check because the customers don't often stick them. In the discount place the customers are apt to stick them. I don't know how you can mix these two approaches. It seems to me it's one way or the other.

Selling is an extension of your own personality, and so it's hard to tell someone else how to do it. But if I had to pick one aspect that is most important in marketing it would be friendliness. If I had to make a choice, I'd rather have a clerk who was less knowledgeable but pleasant. Not fawning or overpowering, but friendly.

Diversification

Although I don't believe you can go both ways, high-end and low-end, you can certainly hedge. The fast-food places now opening for breakfast are doing that, I believe, because I think the morning and the evening customers are two different crowds.

This kind of hedging or diversification can come in various forms. The delicatessen that carries some beer is doing it—a customer who comes in for corned beef for a poker party is likely to buy some beer as well.

And here's how I did it. There were two kinds of nursery school—if the phrase "day care" was used in those days I was not aware of it—when we were in the business: the full-day and the half-day. The full-day school catered to homes in which both parents worked; it was a custodial situation. The half-day school attracted parents who wanted their child exposed to a group situation, or in some cases the mother was working part-time. These were people who wanted their children to have the experiences and advantages of a nursery school and thought a half-day was sufficient.

They were two different kinds of people. The mother who had her child in nursery school all day was frequently going through pain and guilt about it—this was also before the time when most women work—while the half-day mother was probably depriving herself, doing without something, in order to send the child to the school.

Nursery schools catered to one or the other. It was my judgment that I could do both, and we offered both. Now we had a hedge, because the state of the economy had something to do with nursery school business. When the economy dipped, women would go to work, and since we were known for providing a full-day custodial nursery school, we were in business. When the economy took off, the half-day business expanded. People had a little more money, they were willing to give the child a learning experience, and possibly give the mother a little break. In those days we also were known for taking half-day kids. So we did business in both good times and bad.

Self-fulfilling Prophecy

An immigrant came over to this country without a penny to his name. He began to sell hot dogs from a pushcart. He could sell hot dogs so well that soon he had a store of his own and left his pushcart behind. He sold so many hot dogs (although he could barely speak English) that he managed to send his son off to college—Harvard Business School, with some additional graduate work at the Wharton School.

The boy learned a lot there. He came home and said, "Pop, there's a depression on."

"What do you mean, depression?" the father asked.

"People are out of work," the boy explained.

"Is that right?" the father asked.

"Yes, Pop," he said, "and here you are spending all this money on billboards and advertising. We've got to cut back."

"Son of a gun," the father said. "I'm glad I sent that boy to college."

So he cut down on his advertising. The kid was right, because before very long business began to fall off. Realizing then how smart the kid was, the father eliminated all advertising and cut down his hours of operation. He soon found that his business had dropped by 80 percent—just before he went broke.

So don't listen to the doomsayers. Marketing takes its force from the positive approach. People are always calling me to ask whether this is a good time to go into business. They heard that 10 percent of the people are out of work. Well, I respond, how about the 90 percent who are working? One fellow called up, very worried, because he was in business in Houston and the big boom there had ended. I asked him how his business was doing. Fine, he said. Well, what was he worried about?

People get hung up on statistics and the media. Unemployment, the prime lending rate, the consumer price index—all count more with them than their own business judgment. I'm not saying that you fly in the face of all economic reporting. But I'm saying they are not the most important factors. Or to put it another way: if your business is going to hell, does it help that the country's in a boom?

14

Shrinkage

Although burglary is a nuisance to all business, and more than that for some kinds of business and for enterprises located in high-crime areas, it is a mistake to overreact. I keep the doors of my businesses bolted at night, but one hundred pounds of peat moss isn't an item somebody is likely to run to the pawn shop with. The plant shop has been broken into once in the last ten years. Half of my garden stuff is lying outside, and anybody with a pickup truck could run off with it.

I don't have a burglary policy for most of my businesses. Most policies require an alarm system, and some even require a central alarm tied to police headquarters. It would cost a couple of thousand dollars to install, possibly $500 a year to rent the equipment, additional money for the line costs for the alarm system. This might cost me $2,000 a year. If you add up what could be ripped off from my place, it could not come to more than $4,000. I'd be spending a dollar for every two dollars I protected, and that doesn't make economic sense to me. I had much the same attitude about my service station-car rental.

This undoubtedly sounds nonchalant to people in the jewelry business. They deal in the kind of goods that gets fenced. A wholesale cigarette operation ought to have grills on the windows and a burglary policy. A gasoline station has thousands of dollars worth of tools and tires, and might consider burglary insurance. Even the standard business office is replete with the state-of-the-art equipment that would be expensive to replace. But if you consider how much such insurance would cost, it might not pay.

Shoplifting

Retailers find it difficult to get a handle on shoplifting. People have walked out of shops with a hundred-pound statue hidden in a baby carriage, so no matter what you sell you may find shoplifters at work. If the shoplifters can dare that with a statue, you can imagine how much of a target are your cigarettes. The never-ending battle grows more intense every year, but in recent years the retailers in many states have gotten a break. You can question someone inside your store and even have him arrested for reasonable cause with less danger of a false arrest lawsuit, whereas in the past in most states you had to wait for the culprit to leave the store.

The critical point, however, is that shoplifting has to be factored into your prices as an operating expense. Sad but true. Have you ever read indignant stories about how slum dwellers are being cheated because they pay more for groceries? It's true. Any comparison shows that prices are indeed higher in the inner city. That's because the incidence of shoplifting is higher in inner city supermarkets, and the owners have to add in the cost. They also incur other extra costs; for example, the extra worker needed in the truck for deliveries, to guard the truck and its cargo against theft.

Robbery

In our society, a lot of drivers don't want to pick up cash. They don't want to be set up as a target. Drivers in the gasoline delivery business just won't take cash. Nobody wants to be in a position where the criminal element will strike.

I like drop boxes. They're like a little piggy bank set in concrete. Every time your counter person gets a $20 bill—or however you decide to set up the procedure—it goes down the slot into the drop box. They are common in gas stations and all-night stores. Keeping the money safe is only a secondary reason for using a drop box. More important, even the most Neanderthal criminal usually understands that the employees can't get into the drop box and that if he holds the place up the pickings will be small. Even if a lot of money is coming in the door, he can't get at it unless he brings in dynamite. That makes the employees less of a target for robbery.

In case of robbery, your employees ought to be instructed to hand over the money. Never put up an argument with a man with a gun. Up against a gun it should be yessir, nosir, and do you want it gift-wrapped? All they're going to take is money, and that can be replaced.

I don't want any heroes, and I don't want anyone getting shot. Now if you're running a grocery store in a slum area that may be another matter; in that case you may have to stand your ground or you'll be regarded as an easy target. But that's a special case.

The best procedure in my view is to get a drop box and spread the word around that you have one. Some stores even post a notice about it. Every business I've had has used one. They are not expensive, are opened by a combination, and if you sell the business the drop box goes with it, because there is no way you are going to take it with you.

Employee Theft

Employee shrinkage is probably going to be a bigger headache for your business than burglary or robbery. I call it shrinkage because employees don't consider it theft. Taking a box of paper clips or a few ballpoint pens for the kids is not regarded as stealing. Nor is anything stealing that can be eaten on the premises, from a spoonful of ice cream to a quarter-pound of caviar. You may have worked where food was served, and probably ate some, and doubtless didn't regard that as stealing. I know I didn't.

And of course working time—no question but that it's expendable. Few employees would regard getting a haircut on your time instead of on their own time as stealing. Or making a couple of telephone calls—which, if they are toll calls, use both your time and money. You have to keep track of the time your employees put in. A time clock may be too much for a small operation, but when you get past twenty or twenty-five employees it's a must. Or at least have a sign in/out log. It makes your job easier, helps keep track of payroll, and gives you a permanent work record. People don't think they're stealing from you if they come in late.

Stealing merchandise out of the store or office takes a little more rationalizing, but many of your employees will be equal to the task of finding reasons why it is perfectly all right. Running off five hundred copies of a flyer for his kid's school car wash on your photocopier is just being a nice guy, at no cost to himself. As long as it is not money, it isn't really stealing, just helping one's self.

In one of the hospitals I dealt with in my wholesale flower business, some kind of shrinkage was going on. Volunteers served in the flower shop, and the woman in charge of volunteers told me that volunteers do not steal. I disagreed. The hospital director, fortunately, had been brought up in retailing. His father, a pharmacy owner, used to say that he never had a female employee who ever bought stockings or nail polish. For many employees these goods are fringe benefits. You may have to tolerate that, however, because it may be cheaper to do so than to try controlling petty pilferage. So you just write that, too, into the cost of doing business.

When the gasoline shortage struck in 1973, the government was seriously considering allocation based on your previous year's consumption. I asked a woman who worked for me to dig back into the 1972 records and find out how much gasoline was used. I was anxious about what my allocation might be. I quickly learned, however, that I had nothing to worry about. If allocating gas began, I would have enough not only to take care of my business but most of the other businesses for blocks around. I couldn't consume all the gasoline I had coming in allocations if I bought a fleet of tanks. My pumps—sitting out there unlocked during the day and sometimes neglected and left unlocked at night—must have been providing petroleum to the cars of all my employees and most of their friends.

We took precautions, putting in a hidden switch that broke the electrical line and therefore cut power to the pump. I put a lock on the pump, for which even I didn't have a key, gave the control to one person and said he would pump and record and be responsible for all gasoline.

Our gas bills plummeted. The gas shortage of 1973 was one of the best things that ever happened to my business. Even with the skyrocketing gasoline prices, my bills totalled about 40 percent of the preceding year. A perfect example of slovenliness and carelessness, and only one person could be blamed for it—me, the boss. But it taught me a lesson, and I haven't been that sloppy since.

A contractor I know said he doesn't so much mind that half the men in the business used to work for him and learned at his knee, but he resents the way that they climb his fence and help themselves to his supplies when they need them. As ex-employees, they've lost their right to pilfer. But can he afford to hire a guard? Not at $10 an hour he can't.

Even worse than taking merchandise is the hand in the cash register. Your first reaction might be that something is amiss if the register is short. The fact is that you have a bigger problem if the register is over. That means your employee is putting money into the register without ringing it up, and trying to keep track of it. Invariably he loses track of it; if you find the register fairly consistently with more money in it than has been rung up, that's probably what's happening.

Here's what he's doing. A customer comes in and throws down a quarter for a newspaper. Your clerk throws it on the little ledge by the register (the new ones have no ledge for that very reason) and later he sweeps it into the register, computing mentally that he has not rung up 25 cents. When the mental arithmetic hits $20, it's likely that a $20 bill leaves the register and slips into the sock or the pantyhose. But even the best arithmeticians lose track, and end up with something in the register that has not been rung up.

You can check this for yourself with marked money. A $20 bill will leave the register only if a $50 or a $100 comes in. Otherwise it could not go out in change. So if you spike your register with a group of $20s, for which you have the serial numbers, those numbers damn well better be there at the end of the day. Either that or you'd better have some $50s or $100s in there. If any are missing, one of your employees is a hidden partner in your business.

Sometimes customers will tip you that the person who waited on them did not ring up the money. This ought to raise your suspicions.

If you have people making money decisions—buyers or purchasing agents, for example—you might go to one of the professional companies that make background checks. The company would find out for you whether your employee is living at the lifestyle level appropriate to the salary he or she is being paid. Does this employee have any habits, such as heavy gambling or cocaine, that might require a lot of money? Some employers find this offensive, but I don't think you can avoid this kind of check for certain key people, and the cost is not that high.

For the kind of business that deals heavily in cash, or for an employee who handles large amounts of cash, a fidelity bond might be appropriate, available from many insurance companies. Originally written only to cover employee dishonesty, most fidelity bonds now cover any criminal acts, whether employee embezzlement or thefts by outsiders. It also covers check forgery. The insurance company underwriting the bond would investigate any employees covered. Thus a light-fingered employee's adversary becomes not just the boss but a big bonding company with offices in thirty countries. That might discourage theft. If, however, employee theft is not that big a factor in your business, a fidelity bond may be too high priced for you.

So make sure you don't have any partners you don't know about. In some hotel rooms you'll see a little posted sign that says, "Thou shalt not tempt. Don't leave your jewelry and money lying around in the room." That caveat could be applied to your small business. Most people are fairly honest, but don't make it easy to steal from you. Of course there are some people you have to trust, but you should check as much as you can.

Bouncing Checks

A fellow called me lamenting that he had scrimped and saved every penny he could to put it into his business. Then three people gave him bad checks. How can people do this to a small businessman?

If you're in business long enough you can paper your walls with bad checks. Most people who write bad checks for small amounts are not trying to pull something on you. Most likely they are working on a very tight budget. They are hoping to get the check covered before it reaches the bank, and then discover that it can't be done. So the check bounces. What they did was illegal, of course, an indictable offense, and carries a possible prison sentence. But in this society of overworked district attorneys trying to keep up with rapes and murders and child molestation cases and armed holdups, writing a bad check is just not that big a deal to the criminal justice system. If the check-passer doesn't do it too often, or too many times in the same narrow area, nothing may ever happen to him.

There are check services that will guarantee checks. When you call it in, they will run it down for you, and if the check turns out to be no good, they will eat it. The company charges you a percentage for this service. That's one way to do it, but I don't recommend it. However, in some businesses and in some neighborhoods it may make sense to cover yourself that way.

Another way to do it is to eliminate house charges entirely. Don't accept any checks. Operate completely on cash and credit cards. Almost everyone in our society can whip out a Visa or MasterCard at the least.

The problem is that there are a significant number of people who want a house charge. They may not have a credit card or may not want to use it. Or they may not want what they're buying to show up on a credit card, as in the case of a fellow who is buying a bracelet for a woman who is not his wife. Nevertheless, if you're starting a new business, the credit card way is the way to go.

My own experience with bad checks, and with credit cards, has been that we get burned so seldom that it's cheaper *not* to check them. On a credit card check, once I figured how long it takes to have an employee call the company and check on the number, it just didn't pay. (However, new on-line units automatically check the cards for validity.) As for checks, in some stores the employee stamps a rubber stamp on the back and wants to know more about you than is asked on a marriage certificate. All of this waste of employee time over a $16 check doesn't make sense to me.

Say it takes five minutes to do a credit card check or to get the driver's license, social security number, and the rest for a personal check. If you pay your clerk $6 an hour, that comes to $50 of his or her time for every hundred checks. If you didn't do a check and were burned for $35 for every hundred checks, you are still $15 ahead. Now it can be argued that your loss ratio would go up if you eliminated all of these time-wasters. That may be so; the only way to find out is to try. This may sound off-the-wall to you, but I've talked to other businesspeople who have come to exactly the same conclusion. Of course, I'm sure that there are retail operations in other kinds of neighborhoods that would have a much different experience.

During the holiday season, incidentally, things may be different. A lot of people, in a spirit of good will, are spending money they don't have, and at that time credit card checks might be necessary.

Shelf Life

Goods tend to spoil. Even things we regard as nonperishables have a finite shelf life. A ribbon or a candle fades with time. Fashions change. An inventory of wide ties has in a sense stayed around past its allotted shelf life. Most books have to be sold within a certain period of time, or it is no longer worthwhile to keep them in stock. Even paint is only good for a certain finite amount of time.

Dead inventory is as much a drag on your business as spoiled goods. The hardware business, wholesale and retail, is one of those areas in which dead inventory can get away from you. You may pile up tons of it, taking up valuable space. There are places where space is not a problem; but in most parts of the world the ability to use available space profitably is a factor in success. Every square foot of space seems to get filled up eventually. It's better to sell the outdated goods at ten cents on the dollar than to have it sitting there doing nothing and using up space as well. Even if warehousing it is not an expense item, it costs money just to keep track of inventory. So knowing what is hanging around is important. A computer program can help you with that. It can nudge you to recognize that the goods you bought in 1983 are still sitting there on a shelf.

The danger is that you can get lazy. You don't see department stores getting lazy. They are efficient at moving out goods that don't sell. You can show some marketing creativity at getting rid of goods. For instance, a company during the Depression was stuck with a huge shipment of women's shoes that weren't selling. Someone got the idea of cutting out the toes and found they looked good that way—and that they sold quickly. That was the beginning of the open-toed woman's shoe—and my father has been cited in trade magazines as its inventor.

You have to watch how your employees handle the goods. If you're hiring them at minimum wage to pack boxes on the shelf, they will do it the easy way—put them in the front. You have to teach them to rotate the merchandise, to put the new stuff in the back, or you'll always have the oldest goods unsold at the back of the shelf.

Customers damage merchandise. China becomes chipped; dresses get ripped while being tried on, or get perspired onto. Cosmetics are spoiled because someone "tried it on." This is another form of shrinkage.

One of the most important things about shrinkage is being there. The more you're on the scene, the less shrinkage.

I received a call from a fellow who wanted to go into a Quick-Lube business with a couple of his friends. They knew nothing about the business whatever, but they were going to hire a manager. They all worked in the corporate world and none of them wanted to give up the golden parachute. "Our wives will stop in once in a while to see how it's going," he told me.

He's dead in the water. There's nothing wrong with running a business as an absentee owner when you know the business inside out and have a firm grasp of it. But to start it up when you know nothing about it will not work. Furthermore, where can you get someone to run it for you? If the fellow is dishonest, he can steal the store out from under you, and you'll never know the difference. And it's not likely that a person who would take on such a job has the start-up entrepreneurial temperament that's necessary to get a new business going. If he had, he'd be doing it for himself. I'm not going to tell you that it's impossible for a plan like this to work; I'm only going to say it's damn near impossible.

15

Growth

Growth is a two-edged sword. It can be a marvelous opportunity as well as a welcome sign that your business is really taking off. But be careful of growth. The corporate world is littered with the corpses of companies that expanded too quickly.

Whatever the business, there is no such thing as a straight-line growth. Profits and growth do not run in parallel lines to infinity. You may be growing like crazy but the profits may be falling at the same time, and the increase in gross may disguise your growing problem. On the other hand, your profits may be falling and then may take off when you get past a certain barrier. Growth demands sophistication and good judgment to read it right.

One aspect of growth is inarguably a benefit. You already have all kinds of fixed expenses. The liability insurance, the front desk, the electric bill, the rent, all remain the same no matter how much business you do. If you're in the car-rental business, the only real additional expenses for growth are buying and insuring more cars. Everything else is much the same whether you have a fleet of thirty or sixty automobiles. If you have to turn business away because you don't have enough cars, you have a problem. When you turn somebody down for a car that he may have wanted to keep for a month, he will turn elsewhere.

Or suppose you have a barber shop, and you close on Wednesdays and Sundays. The landlord does not say, all right then, you only have to pay five-sevenths of the rent. You have to pay the same amount in dollars per square foot as does anyone else. Nor will your insurance be reduced because you're closed two days a week. Therefore you should grow. You should use your place of business to the maximum.

Some people argue that longer business hours will just spread the customers over a longer time base. I don't believe that. I believe you'll get more business if you stay open longer. If you're the only barber within fifty miles it wouldn't matter, but you are not. Your potential customer may get his haircut while he's at work in another town, because he doesn't get home before five P.M. and doesn't want to spend Saturday in the barber shop.

Some people may have religious objections to working seven days a week, and others may argue that they don't want to be a slave to the business. That's for you to decide; you're your own boss now. But maximizing the use of your overhead is a key to success in business. The difference of 20 hours of use—of your rented office, of your trucks, or of your equipment—could well be the difference between swimming and sinking.

McDonald's is the number-one fast-food franchise in the country, and the top people there know their stuff. A few years ago they said: We have all these golden arches all over the U.S.A., but nobody is buying hamburgers at six in the morning. Yet we have to pay the rent, the insurance, the taxes, the grill is sitting there. It won't cost that much to open at six A.M. But not for hamburgers. And so they came up with the Egg McMuffin. Think about it: everything they make for breakfast—pancakes, Egg McMuffin, sausages, French toast—comes off a grill. They didn't have to add any equipment. All they had to do is come up with some new packaging material. And they got another six hours of use out of their buildings every day. Another sort of person would say, "We're doing great with a business that runs from noon to 11 P.M. What do we want to go into the breakfast world for?" But somebody was bright enough to see the value of Maximizing the Overhead, and got into it. And the other fast-food places have followed suit.

Problems of Growth

Turning down new business hurts, and although you do it, you never get used to it. Few possibilities tempt the beginner more powerfully than a huge contract dangling before his eyes. If I work longer hours, he thinks, if I give up my weekends, hire more people, I can do it. Beware of a big capital investment for equipment to service the supposed lucky break of a big contract.

A major new account means more worker management. Enough people have to be hired to get the job done. But what if you need that large crew only part of the time? You have hired somebody to work a forty-hour week and he's only doing twenty hours of work. Most likely he'll drop into second gear to stretch the twenty hours of work to last forty hours. Isn't that the same thing you'd do, if you were the employee? This will bother you but it's really not his fault, and it's not his problem. It's your problem.

My wholesale flower business went through such a phase a few years back. I received a call from a major supermarket chain, and I visited some executives in their corporate headquarters; the fountains in the lobby impressed me. An executive told me he had taken a look at my operation and liked what he saw, and would I be interested in providing plants and flowers for the supermarket on a nationwide basis?

I found that patently ridiculous. I'd been in the business long enough to know that, even if I had the money to crank up for such a grandiose undertaking, perhaps at an outlay of millions for equipment, I'd then be completely at the mercy of the chain. I'd be their satellite.

So I lowered the proposal. Instead we put together a deal

to supply supermarkets over part of New Jersey. Even this amounted to a lot of additional volume, and every week a few more stores were added to the route.

One day one of my drivers was sick and, unable to find a replacement, I drove the truck myself. After a week of driving, I had seen before my eyes what I should have seen on paper: we were not making any money. We weren't losing money either, but we were spending our time in a profitless project. I had to see it to understand it, just as it's one thing to read about a traffic fatality in a newspaper and another to see it happen in front of you. Everybody else I dealt with was making money—my suppliers, my gasoline salesmen, my drivers—everybody except one guy. I walked away from it. I laid off people, sold a truck, and found that without the chain's business I was making more money. After that revelation I really went on a major housecleaning, ridding myself of all my gift shops and cutting down exclusively to the hospital gift shop business. My volume declined to 30 percent of what I had been doing, but my profit increased by 200 percent. I was doing less business and making more money.

When the opportunity for growth comes along, you have to ask yourself whether it is worth it to you to do so much business. Maybe you would be better off to cut the business back by 10 percent.

If you own a bakery, for example, your one delivery truck can only deliver so much bread in the course of a day—only so much can be loaded in the truck, only so many stops can be made, and so on. At a certain point you are maxed out. You reach that point, and then you get two more customers. If you add another truck, the profit curve is going to plummet. If you figure out the arithmetic, you will see that you now have two drivers and two trucks, making a total of twenty-two stops per day, or an average of eleven per truck. You have reduced your efficiency by almost 50 percent.

That's the way it usually happens. Usually you cannot wait

until you have another twenty customers lined up and then get another truck and another driver. That might happen if you had a hot item and were the only game in town. But usually you have to pop in the new truck and watch your efficiency fall off.

As you get bigger, growth of this sort becomes less of a problem, because if you have two trucks and add a third, you do not lose 50 percent of your efficiency but only a third of it.

Nevertheless, in most businesses, every time you want to grow, your profit curve is going to drop first before it goes up. It's that drop that kills a lot of businesses, if it goes on for too long.

An additional employee for a growing business almost always means a drop in the profit curve. Although it depends upon the business and upon the level of employee, in most cases a new employee is not productive at the beginning of employment. Whatever you're paying him or her is too much. The new employee in terms of profits is often not just worthless but a liability, because not only is he screwing things up, but another employee is using up time training him and correcting his mistakes.

Training people, however, is just another cost of doing business. If you have an office staff of ten and you bring in one new employee, the problem is not that great. But if you have ten and bring in another ten, half your work force is nonproductive and a liability. That's what happens when you overexpand.

Growth can be just what your company needs; it can also be a tempting trap. In my flower business, for example, a truck costs $25,000 and wears out in three years. The minimum for a driver is $300 per week. The truck will run about $100 a week in gasoline, or about $5,000 a year. Insurance costs about the same. That's a lot of cost for growth. In virtually every field a close look reveals the devastation of a company that expanded too quickly, at an artificial pace; the business got away from them. And businesspeople will willingly advise you about the perils of putting all your eggs in one basket.

Growth rarely occurs in a straight line. You have to coast, regroup, get some cash reserves together to tide you over when the roller coaster takes a plunge, as it always does.

Sometimes, though, even when the dollar volume is there, it is not in your best interest to grow. That's a hard lesson to learn—especially if you are young and enthusiastic and ready to go. You can increase your volume by 20 percent while your expenses increase by 26 percent, cutting into your profit margin. Growing involves expenses, and it's rare that expenses pay for themselves right away. The extra expense can prove too much for you. Turning business down is always hard, but sometimes it is necessary.

I wish I had a formula that would answer the question for you whether you should grow or not grow in a given situation. There is no such answer, although there is arithmetic you can do that can determine whether the added volume is going to help you. Remember, however, that there are some advantages in being small. There are a lot of enterprises in which the little guy can beat the big guy. While the little guy may have to pay a little more for material, and loses a little edge there, he doesn't have all the layers of management that the big company has. To a great extent they are about as much advantage as fat to a runner.

Inspections

One story may be enough to illustrate that. We used to get calls from that supermarket chain where we were wholesaling plants. "We're having an inspection at Store 432," the caller would say. That meant we had to get to the store and put in five times more flowers than the store would ever sell.

Everybody else was doing the same thing. The produce man who usually delivered three cases of oranges would bring thirty cases. They wanted a mountain of oranges and a floral display that looked as though a major mobster was being buried.

The supermarket executives would come to the store, march

past this cornucopia of goods, and pronounce that this was really a well-run store. Then they would go away and the store manager would try to figure out what to do with all this super-abundance of produce. Most of it would be thrown away, but that was all right, because the store passed inspection.

Once a week we would get a call to goose the order at one store or another. We were providing plants and flowers on guaranteed sale (which in effect is much like selling on consignment) but I made an agreement with them that all bets were off when this inspection routine came up. I wouldn't pay for the waste.

What shocked me was the sight of a big corporation playing children's games. Do these inspectors really believe what they are seeing? I find it hard to believe that important people at the top of corporate management don't know what a real supermarket looks like, and don't know when they are being shown a fake. Or do they really know, but are playing at some intrigue that means success or failure up at the top of the corporate pyramid? Whatever the explanation, it doesn't spell good news for the stockholders.

Budgeting

I never do much budgeting myself, because I have never tried to look far enough ahead. That is probably a shortcoming in me, but there are some minuses to budgeting. If you have someone working for you and you have budgeted a certain amount for him, he is going to find some way to spend it. If not, you'll cut back his line item the following year.

Some businesses don't budget so much on money figures as on percentages. The manager of a department will be told that five percent of the gross goes to his payroll. If he can run it on three percent, the other two percent is his. "That's because we're willing to spend five percent of the gross on your part of the operation," the manager is in effect being told. "If you want to live with that allocation by working eighty hours a week yourself, fine. If you want to find ways to stimulate your people to higher productivity, fine. We don't care how you do it." My alternative to budgeting has always been: show me a reasonable profit on sales and I'll be happy. Although I have never worked on an annual budget, I have made projections, or worked out a monthly budget—but that's an informal process done privately, usually very late at night, with a calculator.

It will be necessary for you to review your operation regularly, and come up with figures on what you are getting for it.

The Rat Box

My Uncle George knew a lot about how to manage workers. During the Depression, Uncle George bought into a lumber company at a big bargain. The company prospered for many years, and the day came that George, no longer a young man, decided to bow out. With his departure, however, the business soured. His former partner met with him and asked him to come back as a partner, again at a great bargain. With Uncle George back the business flourished again. Then, when he reached his eighties, George retired for good, and the business folded soon afterward. He made the difference between success and failure, and this is how he made it pay.

Like most other enterprises, the lumber business has its peaks and valleys. You have to keep a certain number of men on hand, because when a boxcar comes in it has to be unloaded quickly. You're paying a daily rate for every day it sits on the siding. On the other hand times come up when there's not a whole lot to do around the old lumber yard.

Uncle George knew how to handle that. Right behind the lumber yard stood a pharmaceutical company that used a lot of experimental animals. George had a contract with the company to provide them with animal boxes, which he made out of wood scraps and pieces, at a price that nobody else could match. Every time an employee ran out of work, he was sent to the shed to make rat boxes. That meant *everybody*, office workers as well as yard workers. The rat box detail was always waiting to be done, and George was always six months ahead of himself on orders. Whatever the company needed he could provide.

I hated making rat boxes. I worked for Uncle George for a month while I was home on leave from the Air Force. Hammering away in a hot shed in the middle of the summer held no attractions for me. But it taught me something, nevertheless. I've always had my own equivalent of the rat boxes in all my enterprises—a project that may not even make any money but at least breaks even so that there's always something that pays for my workers' time. In my rental-car business it was always a car that needed a new engine or major repairs. If necessary I would buy a car to have something to work on. I can't afford to lay off my workers and send them home; I'll lose them that way. A rat box in your business can make the difference between profit and loss—something for your employees to do even if it's only marginally profitable.

Uncle George's partner never understood that, which is why the business foundered when George left it. The partner had other business skills—for one thing, he was a great bull-thrower—but he didn't know how to get maximum productivity out of his workers.

16

The Telephone
and Other Tools

Some years ago my wife, in developing a new flower arrangement for the shop, found that the perfect container for it was a spray can cap. How do you find out who makes spray can caps? I can tell you from experience that it is not all that easy. We finally located an Illinois company that made the caps and was willing to sell them to us in the small batches we wanted. We were buying a mere 10,000 caps at a time—a tiny sale to such companies, which are accustomed to dealing in millions. When the Illinois supplier phased this item out we suddenly had to find a new source. I started following leads on the telephone. I called California, New Orleans, Baton Rouge. Finally, somebody on the phone suggested that I try at the Blankola Plastic Company. I had been calling all over the country in pursuit of these caps only to learn that the company I was looking for could be seen from the window of my office! A warehouse was sitting over there in the distance with 40 million spray can caps in it. But I could have driven past that company a thousand times and never known it. Despite its proximity, I found it only by means of the telephone.

I never cease to wonder at how much information can be gathered over the telephone. It may cost you a few dollars. You have to begin with the premise that you don't care what the calls will cost, that you'll persistently follow every lead. Some people can hardly bring themselves to make a toll call, and calling coast-to-coast gives them heart palpitations. I think that's a mistake on their part. I might have been able to develop the same information by letter, but it would have taken a lot more time and effort. I don't understand why people spend so much time on letters when in most cases a telephone call produces an instant response and costs less, when you itemize the *actual* costs of a letter.

I'm a telephone person. I have a telephone in my car and cordless telephones in my home. The telephone is one of the greatest business tools ever developed. As for all its marketing uses, AT&T and its competitors will be glad to help you develop what they call telemarketing.

A good telephone number is impressive and helps business. The best telephone numbers end in double or triple zeros, the numbers that stick the tightest in the memory. But if you call the telephone company and ask for a double-zero number (let's forget triple zeros as perhaps too grandiose for your modest little business) the company will most likely tell you that it has none available. So don't call up cold. You should be ready to rattle off a list of available double-zero numbers not presently in use. You know that all these numbers are available because you have dialed them. You have dialed—or paid someone else to dial— every double-zero number in your telephone exchange. If you know that certain numbers are available and point it out to the telephone company, one of them will probably be bestowed upon you.

"May I Ask Who's Calling?"

I was eavesdropping on a telephone conversation. I took notes; I couldn't help myself. It was the wife of an acquaintance of mine. He is a tailor, but he is also running a personal service and is doing well at it.

I was in the shop when this happened. The boss was not in at the time, and his wife, who also works there, took the call. The first thing she said was that her husband wasn't in. She should never have said that. She should have given the impression that this is a big organization and that she is a secretary or some other kind of employee. Secondly, she told the caller, "He's the only one who can quote rates." When a customer calls about business, the last thing he wants to hear is that nobody there can help him. That's frustrating. The next thing she said is, "Well, I really don't want to beep him right now because he's out making a delivery." Now she has suggested that this is a one-person operation—the boss is out making the delivery himself. She should have said that he was "out on business." Then she suggests: "Why don't you call back later?" Not one little bit is she going to help the customer. She won't take his telephone number and see to it that someone gets back to him later. She did every single thing she could short of insult to burn off the customer.

It was like a training film. I had the fantasy that now she would come back to the telephone and handle the next call the right way, so as to show the wrong way and the right way to do it. But she walked away with a satisfied smile, convinced that she had handled this call in a highly businesslike way.

In many business enterprises the telephone is your lifeline to the world. In our nursery school business, virtually every first contact was by telephone. It's imperative that this first contact be a positive experience. So I developed a canned speech. Everybody with access to the phones had to memorize it, and then repeat it often enough that it no longer sounded like a speech but like normal conversation. Of course everybody worked his or her little changes into it. It went like this:

"At Lane Robbins we don't believe in having things that you readily have at home—swings, seesaws, things like that. Every public park has those. But how many public parks have a real horse and wagon? A tree house? A twenty-eight-foot cabin cruiser? Those are the things that fire the youngster's imagination."

That's how we sold on first contact.

There are some enterprises that don't use telephones. How many people call the local convenience store? For that matter, does the convenience store even have a telephone? Supermarkets usually only have pay telephones. They don't want people calling. Nor do they want their employees making outgoing calls except to order supplies and make other business calls. But they still need a telephone. The boss at headquarters wants to be able to call his employees.

For many businesses, however, without a telephone you might just as well not be in business at all. The caller wants to know how much something costs and whether one is available, your hours, and perhaps even where you are because he may not have an address or needs directions. So the impression made over the telephone is crucial.

I think there are a number of right ways to answer a telephone, but that "hello" is not one of them. Even at home I always say "good morning" or "good afternoon." Some companies just answer by the company name, or say "ABC Company, may I help you?" It's no big thing but it's more pleasant. A rough answer on the telephone and the caller is immediately on the defense.

How to respond properly to a business call is very important to a business. It's amazing how many people pay no attention to it. "Who's calling?" they'll ask; that's a turnoff. I'm offended by it. Here I am, a high-powered executive, and some teeny-bopper is asking me who's calling. "May I ask who's calling?" suggests an entirely different approach. The telephone company has brochures on businesslike telephone techniques, which should be obtained and read.

The interminable holds of telephones are a problem. You get somebody ready to buy your product, then you put him on hold for three minutes. Now he's not only unready to buy but ready to tell you a couple of things.

Your customer in New York calls you in Chicago. Your switchboard answers, "Royal Underwear, please hold," and cuts him off before he has a chance to say anything. Now the meter's running. Not only is he on hold, but hasn't had a chance to open his mouth. The switchboard operator thinks she's doing you a favor, but she isn't. This should never be done. If your switchboard operator is so overworked that she can't take a few more seconds to avoid irritating a customer, you've got a problem. Maybe you have to add another operator.

There are non-telephone people. Although some people can practically make love to a telephone, other people choke up after a few words. You have to take this into account when you are hiring if your whole business comes over the telephone.

If your business does come over the telephone, many of the responses to calls have to be thought out in advance and taught, so that questions are answered in the right way. The caller asks, "How much are a dozen roses?"

One answer: "Fifteen dollars."

Another answer: "Our long-stemmed roses are fifteen dollars a dozen. This includes a box, with the roses surrounded by baby's breath and baker fern, wrapped in tissue paper, sealed with a large red ribbon, and of course a card of your choice."

There's a lot of difference between those two answers—the difference between somebody who's selling roses over the telephone and a clerk.

More and more people are conditioned to the idea that they don't have to pay for a telephone call. If your business draws from a wide area, you're at a disadvantage if your customers have to make a toll call to reach you. Even if you don't have a nationwide business, but are doing business over an area of seven or eight counties, you might need an 800 number, because some people won't place an order if it means a toll call. Even I'm swayed, and I'm as reconciled to toll calls as anyone I know; if I'm looking for a flight, and one airline company has an 800 number and the other does not, I'll call the 800 number first. You can buy an 800 number for a single state and for a multiple number of states.

When You're Out

The answering machine in the last few years has come along as a widely used alternative to the answering service, and it costs less. Yet an answering machine can aggravate those people for whom a 25-cent telephone call is a big deal and a long-distance call a major investment. When one of them gets an answering machine, it may cost you a customer.

Still, I prefer the machine to an answering service. The service is always putting the caller on hold, and when the service gets back to the caller, it usually can't be of much help. The reason is because answering services are generally understaffed, but if they hired more people the rates would go up.

Some people use those beepers that tell you someone is trying to reach you via telephone. That's a little too much for me. If I were a brain surgeon it might make sense to try reaching me when I'm on the golf course, but in my business it isn't usually a question of life or death.

If you have an office but are home a lot, you can run a tie line to your home and receive business calls there.

Beginners often use their home telephone for business. That may be a necessary expedient for a rank beginner, but the telephone company does not allow that as the rate structure is higher for a business telephone. The telephone company does not actively go looking for trespassers, but I heard from a fellow who put a business sign out in front of his house with the home phone number on it, and somebody at the telephone company found out about it. They were going to have his phone pulled.

As soon as you get to be an enterprise of any size you'll want to advertise; you may want to be in the Yellow Pages, and you'll want to be listed as a business in the White Pages. You can't do any of these things unless you have a business telephone.

Owning Phone Equipment

The days of renting phone equipment are part of the past, back with black-and-white television. People were not aware of it then because it was packaged in with the rest of the telephone bill. Why pay $700 a year rent for telephone equipment when for a little more every month you can finance new equipment and at the end of two or three years it will be paid up?

This is one area, however, in which you should make certain that you're buying the best. You can always tell when someone is talking on a cheap telephone. In business that's particularly bad, because when a customer is straining to hear he is on edge and in no mood psychologically to be sold anything. When you price telephone equipment, remember that this is something that will be around for some time.

TECHNOLOGY

There are all kinds of office and store technical equipment now. Your attitude toward keeping up technologically should be open but careful. There are cash registers available now that practically do your bookkeeping for you. Some are almost mistake-proof.

The cash registers in the fast-food stores are like that. When you ask for five hamburgers, two French fries, and one hot chocolate, that's how it's rung up. Not the amounts, but the items. The cash register shows how much each item costs and tells the clerk how much change to give back. It also tells the owner what items are moving, and sometimes what time of the day they are moving.

That may be great for your business. But they are expensive cash registers, and you may not be able to use all this data to any purpose. You may not be a big enough statistical sample to take advantage of the information generated.

Furthermore, you can become so dependent on data that you lose touch with your instincts. Customers may be coming into your diner because you have a blond waitress who looks great in a sweater. All the statistics in the world won't tell you that. If the figures show your business dips on Tuesdays and Wednesdays, you may sit puzzling over this for a long time and never realize that it's the blonde's days off.

There are also scales that show prices for you. These may be luxuries you can't afford. I usually work with a small enough profit margin that I can't justify these items. They may be necessities, especially if you don't have intelligent employees. But if you ever go to a bankruptcy sale and see all the fancy technology up for sale, you may be seeing why the business went broke. A used showcase would have done the job just as well. Why buy an expensive lift if you only have to put up a car once every couple of weeks? Why buy a wrecker if you don't use it that often? These are the questions a beginner working on tight money has to look at carefully. Jerry-rigging some method may be your answer—or bankruptcy sales, used equipment sales, or asking around the trade for a used item. Try the oddball sources.

Business Cards

Get them. People ask for them, and some people keep business card files. If you don't have a card you don't make the file.

I like top-quality business cards. Spend some money on them. Don't get a business card that looks as though a high school freshman printed it as his first print-shop training project. Get one with a couple of colors and embossed or with an embossed look—but understated. It's always the people with one-person operations who have the cards with their names in 18-point type. The understated, quality card is most impressive.

Letterheads

The same goes for letters. There's no substitute for good-quality stationery in a good-quality envelope. I always open those first when I'm opening mail. You want something that will set you a little apart—off-white, or gray, or blue. For a while I had an odd-sized envelope so that when a pile of envelopes was stacked mine stood out like a shaved card in a deck. Those kinds of envelopes are opened quicker. It doesn't cost that much more to get top quality.

If I can avoid it, I don't answer letters, at least not with another letter. I call. For a small business, it will cost you more to write a letter than to make a call. On the other hand, if you're notifying somebody that if he doesn't do A, you are going to do B, a letter leaves a record, a phone call doesn't. Keep carbons or photocopies. If there might possibly be legal trouble later on, send the letter by certified mail and keep the receipt.

Sometimes I respond to letters by writing on the original letter and mailing it back, especially if it's a very non-personal kind of query. Some people are offended by this, but I have to risk offending them. It saves me time.

Although I don't write many letters, I do write thank-you notes. On the day after a business meeting I often write something like this: "Hey, Sam, it was great getting together with you yesterday. Thanks for your thoughts." Etc. Most people don't do this, so when I do it I'm a little different. It brings the relationship a little closer.

I'm beginning to think that there's an advantage in providing a return envelope with bills. As a bill-payer I like getting one; it's one less thing for me to think about. As a bill-receiver there's an advantage in knowing without opening the envelope that it's a check. Save steps by using window envelopes for bills.

You should have a letterhead and envelopes with a return address that matches the motif of your letterhead, but you should also have cheap, plain, supermarket envelopes and a rubber stamp for your return address. There's no point in sending out the payment for your gas bill in an impressive envelope.

Sales Slips, Invoices, and Other Paper

Keep it simple. Don't use carbon paper, but NCR paper, which makes copies without the mess of carbon; and if you don't need three copies don't get three-copy paper. One deficiency in our business operation was taking telephone messages; they'd end up on all sorts of little scraps of paper. So I bought a message book that provides a second copy of phone memos. Three months later I can refer to it and see who called at what time. It is very useful. And it saves a lot of lost messages.

Small companies have a great communications advantage just by virtue of being small. If I worked in big business, you wouldn't have to pay me: just give me the photocopy concession. Somebody writes a memo: "I'll be out of town for two days. Here's my telephone number." Take a look at the list of where this memo went—it went to everybody but the cleaning people. Maybe that's necessary, but what an expense of time and paper.

TRADE SHOWS

Another important tool of which you should avail yourself is trade shows. For the businessperson it doesn't cost, it pays to go to them. All the arguments against them—I can't afford the time; I probably won't find anything; I don't like going to the big city; it costs too much to fly all that distance—don't really make business sense.

If you don't go to trade shows in your field you're giving your competitor a leg up. In two or three days you can see more products than if salesmen were waiting to see you in a line five blocks long. Furthermore, you see them in a competitive environment, pitted against one another. You keep up with what's new and what's available. You can depend on it that your competition will be there, so why not you?

It's amazing how many businesspeople penalize themselves by not attending trade shows because they don't like cities or find the shows confusing. It only takes a little research to find the important trade shows nearest you. If you live in one of the major metropolitan areas you have an advantage because there are only a few important cities for the big shows—New York, Chicago, Dallas, Los Angeles, and maybe San Francisco. And why not take a perquisite for yourself that is a perfectly legitimate business deduction?

In most cases you need credentials to get into trade shows. Sometimes a business card is enough. Find out what you need to get in before you go there. And if for some reason you want to get into a trade show outside of your field, all you need is to get a printer to make you a business card; nobody ever questions a card. Then you can get a badge with the name of your company printed on it (even if the company does not exist). There's nothing fraudulent about this. The credentials requirement is just to keep casual strollers out of the show and to restrict it to people with a serious interest.

Some trade shows are expensive to attend, however. In order to get into some of them you have to be registered as attending an annual convention of the trade. And registration may cost a couple of hundred dollars. I would be the last person to tell anyone that he or she should borrow someone else's credentials to get in. Let me just say that I think you have to be inventive.

If you want to go to an expensive trade show, you might be able to share the cost with a couple of your competitors. One of you registers and the others take turns using his badge. Nobody ever asks you for cross-identification when you go in; all you need is a badge. There's a man in a blue suit who checks your badge. So the three happy competitors all get a look at the big show; one goes in the opening morning, one goes in for the afternoon, and the third goes in for the closing day.

Conventions are important too. Not all conventions are whoopee cushions and secret handshakes. I think they're so important that I have it written into my contract with NBC that I attend the two big industry conventions every year. At a convention you get to meet your competition and exchange ideas in a social setting. That's important. One of my basic rules, you recall, is don't reinvent the wheel. If you're wrestling with a problem, it's possible that thirty other people in the business have solved the same problem after much work. Why should you be the thirty-first? Go to the convention workshops and you may find the solution without working for it.

At trade shows, and sometimes at conventions too, you will often find either an official or an unofficial bulletin board where people tack up their business cards. This can be a good source for you. If you want to become a manufacturer's representative a trade show is a great place to make contacts—or as the current phrase has it, to do some networking. It's also a good place to look if you're in search of a manufacturer's representative for your own products. You may find dozens of people looking for certain lines to represent.

Say you make some sort of special toy—handmade puppets, for example. At a toymakers' convention not only will you find people who want to represent you, but their business cards will probably mention what regions they cover. There might be no other way you'd ever locate that person.

The one other place you might find a representative is a little classified advertisement in a trade magazine. And trade publications are also indispensable to your business. Events are happening all the time that pertain to your business, and they are thoroughly covered only in trade publications. All kinds of common situations for people in the trade come up in these magazines. It's another tool to help keep you from reinventing the wheel. In the trade magazines you will learn about the solutions that others have worked out to problems that you face.

Trade organizations are important as well, for many of the same reasons. In many professions as varied as financial planning and medicine, it's absolutely necessary for you to keep current. These are not static fields; something innovative is happening in them all the time. Conditions change constantly in almost every business. Even if you reproduce fourteenth-century manuscripts, new techniques in improved reproduction are occurring all the time. You can't keep up with these events unless you go to trade shows and conventions, read trade publications, and belong to trade organizations.

KNOW YOUR COMPETITION

There's another advantage in keeping up with the trade: knowing your competition. As much of what has been said in these pages shows, I'm a strong believer in that.

If you own a shoe store, you should be able to name every competitor in your trade area. And what market they cater to. And where they stand in the pecking order—who's first, who's second, and who's way back in the pack. And most important, why they are first or second or far in the rear.

You have to know them and what they are selling. Not because you are going to price against the competition, necessarily, but because it may mean you will have to change your business. Some people conduct business with the notion: I don't care what others are doing, I'm doing my own thing. There's a certain validity in that, but even so you have to know as much about your competitor as you can find out: what's his market, where he's buying, what he's buying, what are his strengths and weaknesses, and how does this affect you.

If you're in the shoe business, and there are fifteen other shoe stores in the area, you should have been in every one of them. Your employees ought to visit them from time to time and see what's going on. You or, if you don't have time, your spouse or one of your employees should look regularly through the local newspaper and see who's advertising shoes. You may not like rock and roll but if you're selling shoes to young people, somebody in your vast organization ought to be listening to the rock stations to hear if there are any shoe ads on them. And if one of the shoe stores is advertising regularly, and you know enough about this competitor to know that he or she is not stupid, some money must be coming out of that advertising. So maybe your ads belong on those stations. You may not like that kind of music but that's what your customers listen to. You may think the local newspaper is the best paper in the world, but the best place to put your advertisements may be a newspaper you don't like at all. That will help your business succeed. Don't let your own preferences blind you to the facts.

17

Good Luck

I got out of the nursery school business too late—probably five years too late. A young man who was working for the municipality in which I was an official had approached me expressing an interest in buying the business. He said he had always wanted to be in that business and had the right background but not the capital. One day when I was feeling clearheaded I picked up the telephone and called him.

"If you can get over here in less than half an hour, I'm going to make you an offer you can't refuse," I told him. "If it takes you more than a half-hour I probably will have changed my mind."

He was there in twenty minutes. I made a proposal to him that he accepted on the spot.

I was completely serious about the fact that I might change my mind in a half-hour, because I was offering him a deal for no money down. I considered it because I had the feeling he had the ability to bring it off. Other people had made offers with money down, but I had never been persuaded that I'd ever see any more money after the down payment; I was afraid they might milk it or destroy it. This young man, however, appeared to have the motivation and the desire. He was exactly the age I had been when I started the business, and he was ambitious and hungry.

These qualities were more important to me than whether he had been able to put some money away.

If the time ever comes when you decide to get out of the business, there are a lot of considerations but only one all-important one: the buyer.

Not, of course, if you're blessed with a straight cash deal. In that case it doesn't matter who's buying it, and you have no need to care. But cash deals, particularly in these times, happen so seldom. The likelihood is that you will have to carry your successor's paper, just as your predecessor probably carried your paper for several years. You will have to cover yourself as best you can with chattel mortgages and the like, but let's be honest—you're taking a chance. Selling an enterprise is taking a big chance, just as buying an enterprise is. And if you get burned, you get burned. That's what business is like. You assess your buyer closely and use your best judgment.

My buyer worked out fine. I carried him for a long time, he met every payment on time, and eventually he paid me off. If it happens to you, I hope you do as well.

The Two Kinds of Businesspeople

We've talked before about how the entrepreneur and the manager—the two basic kinds of businesspeople—are seldom both found in the same body. If you're an entrepreneurial type, you're probably going to become sick of your business after a while. It happens relatively quickly, unless there's a constant, changing panorama. Going to the office every day and knocking out the work is a skill of organization man, managerial man. And that kind of man (or woman) is absolutely essential to a mature business.

For the entrepreneur, who isn't really interested in operating mature businesses, the trick is to know when to get out. That's something only he or she knows, but it's usually pretty soon. The romance is short. The entrepreneur conceives it, gets it afloat, gets it profitable, and abandons ship—turns it over to someone else.

If your business has become a corporation of some size, you may not even have to do that; you can depend on it that the managers will get rid of you. It's a classic business story that the great entrepreneur who starts the company eventually gets tossed out. He really doesn't fit in anymore. He doesn't have the ability to make the business grow. That seems to be the job of bean counters and numbers crunchers. They couldn't have done what the entrepreneur did—they lack the ability to conceptualize and to take the bold risks that are necessary. But they are just the people who can take a business with a strong foothold and make something out of it. Some enterpreneurs understand this and bow out gracefully; others find it impossible to accept and have to be dragged out kicking and screaming.

Trendy Stuff

There are always trendy businesses, and in these fields particularly the entrepreneur should get on top of the trend, make his profits while the trend is hot, and get out before it cools off. Back in the 1930s one of the trendy businesses was miniature golf courses. For a while there was one on every other street corner. The miniature golf course is still around, of course, but is found only in recreation centers now. In the 1950s the trendy business was the jump center, or pit trampolining, as it was called. I'm sure insurance coverage had something to do with their short life as a trend. Then there was the hula hoop, the mood ring, the pet rock, which have disappeared, and indoor tennis, which is still popular but has levelled off from its phenomenal growth of a decade ago. Some of those tennis courts are car dealerships now.

If you're going to get into trendy enterprises, get in early, and, even more important, get out early. The sheep who get shorn are the ones who get into it right at its peak. They pay top dollar for the business, watch the money come in by the truckload for a short time, get the feeling that it's going to last forever, and quickly discover how wrong they were.

Trends are to some extent dependent on other conditions. One of the reasons fancy ice cream parlors are so popular now, featuring expensive brands and exotic (even made-to-order) flavors, is the great burden that saloons are laboring under. The liability insurance costs are so high that ice cream just seems a lot less complicated to the small retailer.

Final Thoughts

Before closing, I want to make sure that I have impressed you with the enormous importance of your employees. When you have a good employee, keep him or her happy and involved. And try to give them incentives.

Almost everywhere you look, from the corner store to the Fortune 500, disincentives are at work. As long as the game is played so that there's no incentive to stick his or her neck out, the employee is going to play it safe. The insurance underwriter will turn down a risk because that's the safest course. There's no reward for risk but there's always a penalty for failure. Companies lose business because the employees want to go along with the status quo. If your manager never is rewarded when he makes a smart buy, but you're always on his case when he makes a mistake, he doesn't have any incentive to give anything a try. Employers often say, why should I pat him on the back just for doing his job? That's what he's paid to do. If your business is going to be successful, it will need successful employees, and you will have to stop disincentives and turn them into incentives.

I'm still waiting to meet the really successful person who works a forty-hour week. Maybe later, when they have the business in place and everything running smoothly, they take some time to spend a few weeks on the yacht. But everybody I've ever heard of who makes big money, unless it was inherited, works extremely hard for it—at a pace that a lot of people can't match.

Not because they lack the physical equipment, but because they lack the mind-set.

Keep yourself healthy. You wouldn't let your truck go out with no oil in the engine because you know the engine will be damaged. But the same guy who insists that the oil be checked every morning won't take the time to get a physical checkup. The older you get the more important it is that you take care of these things. You have to be smarter when you're older because the kids have more energy. One way to husband those resources is to keep yourself fit.

You ought to think of your health as your base, not as a blessing among others but the one upon which all the others are based. But if you find that too difficult, think of yourself as a commodity. The people at NBC are concerned about my health. I'm sure one of the reasons is basic human sympathy, but the main reason is that they see me, and my colleagues, as products. If I fall off a cliff, it's going to be costly to replace me. Exactly the same thing is true of your business. If you become ill it may be the death of your business. So if you don't owe it to yourself, you owe it to your business to take reasonable care of yourself. That means getting enough sleep to keep your health up, keeping your weight down, and not drinking to excess. Drink has destroyed a lot of once-healthy businesses.

People do lose energy as they get older, but I'm not persuaded that it has to be that way. I'm convinced that I can run rings around most of the people half my age. That doesn't mean I can get suited up and beat them at football, but in terms of work I can do it. I mean getting on an airplane, riding three thousand miles, getting off to do six interviews and two shows, then going out drinking afterward, then getting up three hours after going to bed and doing the whole thing over again.

Most of that is not physical at all, but mental. When I'm home doing a show in New York, I can sleep seven or eight hours, just like everyone else. But I can do without a lot of sleep and work at a grueling pace because I'm conditioned to it. Being smarter than the other fellows helps a little, but I don't think I'm a whole lot smarter. But I do know that I can work a lot harder than most people. And that's what makes the real difference.

Maybe that's not entirely a good trait because sometimes we sacrifice something of the quality of life in keeping our noses always to the grindstone, or so the philosophers and the songs tell us. But if you want the material things in life that's the way to get them.

Good luck, my friends, and I hope you do get them.

Index

Accountants
functions of, 41, 123, 124, 142,
184-86
selection of, 123-24
Accounting, creative, 124
Accounts payable, 43
Accounts receivable, 43
Advertising
and appealing copy, 210-11
for start-up money, 87-90
in relation to franchising, 70
need for repetition, 211-12
television, 62
White Pages, 249
Yellow Pages, 209-10, 213, 249
Alcohol, and the businessperson,
261
Anticipation, 195
Apprenticeship, 17-18
Attorneys
functions of, 35, 43-44, 99,
117-19, 156
selection of, 118-19
Auditing your sales, 40

Bank
commercial accounts, 116-17

co-signers on loans from, 91
FDIC, 84
loans from, 32, 83-85
selection of, 110-15
Bank checks, overdrawn, 112, 201,
227-29
Banking, electronic, 115
Bankruptcy, key to, 14-15
Billing, 201-2
Blue Sky. See Good will
Board of Health, 149
Bond, fidelity, 226-27
Bond, performance, 32
Bookkeeping, 185-86. See also
Accountants
Brand identification, 70
Brokerage house, discount, 216-17
Brokerage house, full-service,
216-17
Burnout, 37
Business
location selection of, 33-35
mail order, 61-62, 67
misconceptions about, 13-28
purchasing of a, 39-41
selling of a, 258
start-up of, 44-49

Business cards, 250-51, 253, 254
Businessperson, two types
  Type One, 30-31, 37
  Type Two, 30-31
Buying
  at a discount, 195
  from the manufacturer, 194
  in large quantities, 193-94

Cash registers, 249-50
Certificate of occupancy, 158
Competition, 175-78, 255-56
Computers, value of, 190-91, 229
Consumer Price Index, 40
Contractor, independent, 137
Contributions, political, 160
Conventions, 254
Corporation, 102-5, 150, 165.
  See also Subchapter S
Corporation charter, 104-5
Corruption, political, 161-62
County clerk, office of, 100
Covenants, restrictive, 41-42
Credit cards, 202-5
  American Express, 203-4
  and employee's tip, 205
  as vehicle to borrow money, 91
  Diner's Club, 203
  Discover Card, 203
  MasterCard, 201, 203, 228
  VISA, 201-4, 228
Customer lists, 41. *See also*
  Good will
Customers, treatment of, 14, 216
Customer service, 216

Deep Pockets, 165
Defer payments, 96
Department of Commerce, Small
  Business Administration, 90-91

Depreciation deduction for tax
  purposes, 31-33
Drop boxes, 223

Employees
  age factor of, 128-29
  as assets, 14
  delegation of responsibility to,
    168-69
  disincentives for, 260
  estimating costs of benefits for,
    15
  expectations of, 130-31
  hiring, 127-30
  off-the-books, 137-38
  part-time, 138-39
  personality of, 21-22
  perquisites, 136-37
  referrals from, 129
  self-employed, 184
  skills of, 57-58
  subterfuges, 137-38
Enterprises, trendy, 259-60
Entrepreneurs, part-time
  problems of, 25-27
Entrepreneur type, 258-59
Envelopes, window, 252
Equipment, obtaining new and
  used, 46-47
Escrow agent, 44
Escrow arrangement, 44
Expansion, 233
  problems of, 235-38
Expenses, decreasing, 96-98

Family, and the businessperson,
  145-47
Favors, 106
Federal Trade Commission, 75
Floor layout, 45-46

Floor-planning, 197
Franchisee, 69
Franchising
   advantages of, 69-72, 76-77
   disadvantages of, 72-77
Franchisor, 69
   assistance from, 70-71
Front-end displays. *See*
   Merchandising

Gimmicks. *See* Marketing
Good will, 41-42
Government regulations, 17, 75-76,
   151, 152-60. *See also* Licensing

Health, and the businessperson,
   261
Home, as business location, 178
Homeowner's line of credit, 84,
   115-16. *See also* Bank
Homestead Law, 83-84
Husband and Wife as business
   partners, 147

Incorporation, 99, 102-3
Insurance, liability, 120-21, 149
Insurance, life
   borrowing on, 86
Insurance, property, 119-20
Insurance agent, selection of,
   121-23
Internal Revenue Service, 32, 33,
   39, 40, 89-90, 102, 103, 117, 124,
   137, 187-88
Inventory
   amount of, 196-97
   dead, 229
   purchases, 40
   records, 188-89
   See also Shrinkage

Job, buying a, 64
Jobs, checklist of likes and dislikes,
   53-55
Job-sharing, 138-39

KISS (Keep it Simple, Stupid),
   182-83
Knowing your strengths and
   weaknesses, 19-20

Language, offensive, 60-61
Leases, 43-44
   advantages of, 35
   buy-out clause, 36
   disadvantages of, 35-37
   miscellaneous obligations and,
   36
Letterhead stationery, 251-52
Liability, 32, 44, 99, 105
   as an asset, 94-95
   product, 149, 164-66
Licensing, 160-62. *See also*
   Government regulations
Loans, from family members,
   85-86; from seller, 86-87;
   See also Bank; Department of
   Commerce, Small Business
   Administration
Location of business, and the
   franchise, 72

McDonald's, 234-35
Mailing lists, 41. *See also*
   Good will
Mail order business, 61-62
Managerial type, 258-59
Marketing, 207-20
   diversification, 218
   friendliness, 218
   gimmicks, 208-9, 215-16

multi-level, 62-64
Merchandising, 214
  cleanliness and, 216
Money, underworld, 88-89
Mortgage, home
  borrowing from, 92-93

Names, trade, 165
NCR paper, 252
New York Times, 87-88

One-person operation, 64-65
Operating your business, precepts
  on, 167-80
Overhead, 200-201, 234
Owner, managing store on
  premises, 38

Packaging and labeling
  regulations, 150. *See also*
  Government regulations
Partners, general, 102
Partnership, limited, 102
Partnerships, 101-2
Payroll records, 184
Pennysaver, 210
Pension plan
  borrow from, 86
Police, and the businessperson,
  152-53
Politicians, and the businessperson,
  125-26
Predictability of franchise, 69-70
Pricing, 197-201
Profit, gross, 14
Profit curve, 237
Proprietor, sole, 101
Purchasing an established business,
  37-44
  checklist of considerations, 42-43

Pyramid scheme, 63

Real estate transaction, 44
Record-keeping, 181-91. *See also*
  Bookkeeping; Accountants
Registration of trade names,
  100-101
Remembering names, importance
  of, 106
Renting a business, tax advantages
  of, 31-33
Replacement, and the indisposed
  businessperson, 140
Retailer, description of, 58-59
Right of First Refusal, 76
Risk-taking, 27-28
Robbery, 221, 222-23
Rubber stamp, 257

Sales gross, 14
Sales, retail, 215
Salesmen, 208
Saving money for capital, 93-94
Self-motivation, 167
Selling a business, reasons for,
  37-38
Shelf Life, 229
Shoplifting, 222
Shopping malls, business within,
  36-37
Shrinkage, 38, 223, 230
Sign in/out log, 224
Skill, three kinds
  flexibility, 56-57
  knowing your field, 55-56
  self-discipline and flexible hours,
  58
Small Claims Court, 201
Subchapter S, 103-4
Supplies, available from
  franchisors, 71

Tax deductions, 33, 186-88. *See also*
    Depreciation deduction for tax
    purposes; Internal Revenue
    Service
Tax evasion, 40
Tax records, sales, 184
Telephone
    choice of service, 196
    double zero number, 244
    800 number, 247-48
    equipment ownership, 249
    etiquette, 246
    use of, 243-44
Telephone answering machine, 248
Telephone answering service, 248
Television, late-night advertising
    on, 62
Theft, employee. *See* Shrinkage;
    Robbery
Time, organization of, 22-25,
    169-70
Time clock, 224

Tipping, 105, 139
Trade organizations, 255
Trade publications, 254-55
Trade shows, 252
Treasury bill rate, 40
Turnover, 200

Underpricing, 198
Uniform Franchise Offering
    Circular, 75

Venture capital, 83

Wall Street Journal, 87-88
Weighing your product, 150. *See
    also* Government regulations
Wholesaler, description of, 58-59

Zoning, 149, 153-57
Zoning Board of Adjustment,
    153-54